Fodor's POCKET

T5-AFS-412

são paulo

first edition

fodor's travel publications
new york • toronto • london • sydney • auckland
www.fodors.com

contents

maps

on the road with fodor's

THE MORE YOU KNOW BEFORE YOU GO, the better your trip will be. The city's most fascinating small museum or its best restaurant could be just around the corner from your hotel, but if you don't know it's there, it might as well be across the globe. That's where this guidebook and our Web site, Fodors.com, come in. Our editors work hard to give you useful, on-target information. Their efforts begin with finding the best contributors—people with good judgment and broad travel experience—the people you'd poll for tips yourself if you knew them.

Karla Brunet is a photographer and designer who studied art in San Francisco and who teaches digital photography in Brazil. A language major, she not only speaks Portuguese, but also English, Spanish, and French. Her major passion is travel, and she has done a great deal of it in the Americas, Europe, and Asia. Her most recent expedition took her to the Inca sites in Ecuador, Peru, and Bolivia.

Joyce Dalton, who contributed to Practical Information, has been traveling for more years than she cares to count. Her travel articles and photos appear in numerous trade and consumer publications. Joyce also has revised chapters for *Fodor's South America* and *Fodor's Eastern and Central Europe.*

Don't Forget to Write...

Keeping a travel guide fresh and up-to-date is a big job. So we love your feedback—positive and negative—and follow up on all suggestions. Contact the Pocket São Paulo editor at editors@fodors.com or c/o Fodor's, 280 Park Avenue, New York, New York 10017. And have a wonderful trip!

Karen Cure

Karen Cure
Editorial Director

são paulo

In This Chapter

Updated by Karla Brunet

introducing
são paulo

CROWDED BUSES GRIND DOWN streets spouting black smoke, endless stands of skyscrapers block the horizon, and the din of traffic deafens the ear. But native *paulistanos* (inhabitants of São Paulo city; inhabitants of São Paulo State are called *paulistas*) love this megalopolis of 17 million. São Paulo now sprawls across 7,951 square km (3,070 square mi), 1,502 square km (580 square mi) of which make up the city proper. The largest city in South America makes New York City look small.

In 1554 Jesuit priests, including José de Anchieta and Manoel da Nóbrega, founded the village of São Paulo de Piratininga and began converting Indians to Catholicism. Wisely set on a plateau, the mission town was protected from attack and was served by many rivers. It remained unimportant to the Portuguese Crown until it became the departure point for the *bandeira* (literally, "flag") expeditions, whose members set out to look for gemstones and gold, to enslave Indians, and, later, to capture escaped African slaves. In the process, these adventurers established roads into vast portions of previously unexplored territory. São Paulo also saw Emperor Dom Pedro I declare independence from Portugal by the Rio Ipiranga (Ipiranga River), near the city.

In the late 19th century, São Paulo became a major coffee producer, attracting both workers and investors from many countries. Italians, Portuguese, Spanish, Germans, and Japanese put their talents and energies to work. By 1895, 70,000 of the 130,000 residents were immigrants. Their efforts transformed the place from a sleepy mission post into a dynamic financial and cultural hub. Avenida Paulista was once the site of many a coffee baron's mansion. Money flowed from these private domains into civic and cultural institutions. The arts began to flourish, and by the 1920s São Paulo was attracting such great artists as Mário and Oswald de Andrade, who introduced modern elements into Brazilian art.

In the 1950s, the auto industry began to develop and contributed greatly to São Paulo's contemporary cityscape. In the past 30 years, people from throughout Brazil have come seeking jobs, many in the Cubatão Industrial Park—the largest in the developing world—just outside the city limits. Today, like many major European or American hubs, São Paulo struggles to meet its citizens' transportation and housing needs, and goods and services are expensive. Yet, even as the smog reddens your eyes, you'll see that there's much to explore. As a city committed to making dreams come true, São Paulo offers top-rate nightlife and dining and thriving cultural and arts scenes.

The city faces the Atlantic shore in the southeast region of the state that shares its name. From town it's easy to travel by car or bus to the state's many small, beautiful beaches and beyond to the states of Paraná, Rio de Janeiro, and Minas Gerais. Although most sandy stretches are a couple of hours from the city, good side trips can be as close as the 30-minute drive to Embu.

PLEASURES AND PASTIMES

DINING

With more than 12,000 restaurants and a melting pot of cultures, there's a cuisine for every craving. Japanese and Italian restaurants abound. Indeed, paulistanos are very proud of their pizza, especially pies topped with mozzarella, arugula, and sun-dried tomatoes. Establishments that serve Portuguese, German, French, and Spanish dishes are also popular. Be sure to try the *beirute*, a popular Lebanese contribution that's like a Middle Eastern submarine sandwich, served hot in toasted Syrian bread and sprinkled with oregano.

Of course many restaurants offer traditional Brazilian specialties such as *feijoada* (the national dish of black beans and a variety of meats), *churrasco* (barbecued meats), and *moqueca* (fish stew made with coconut milk and *dendê*, or palm oil). Some places specialize in regional food from Bahia (whose spicy dishes are often toned down), Minas Gerais, and elsewhere. *Virado à paulista* (beans, eggs, and collard greens) is a typical São Paulo dish. Nothing goes better with Brazilian food than a *caipirinha* (a drink with the rumlike *cachaça*, lemon, and sugar).

LODGING

You'll find many world-class hotels here; most are in big buildings on or around Avenida Paulista. Regardless of the price category, most hotels have good restaurants and buffet breakfasts.

NIGHTLIFE

From romantic garden terraces where you can grab a quiet drink to clubs where you can dance to throbbing techno music till dawn, the nightlife reflects the city's eclectic heritage. The chic and wealthy head for establishments, many of which serve food, in the Vila Olímpia and Itaim neighborhoods. The Pinheiros neighborhood, near Vila Madalena, has a large concentration of Brazilian clubs and alternative bars. The neighborhood of Jardins has some of the city's best dance clubs as well as a selection of gay and lesbian bars.

São Paulo's music clubs often feature jazz and blues artists. On weekends you'll find samba and *pagode* (musicians sitting around a table playing for a small crowd) in clubs throughout the city. At *forró* couples dance close to the fast beat and romantic lyrics of music that originated in the country's northeast. Forró has become quite popular in the past few years.

PARKS AND GARDENS

In Latin America's biggest urban park, Parque Ibirapuera, you can ramble for an entire day without seeing all the grounds, museums, and cultural attractions. On Sunday, you may well be accompanied by thousands of paulistanos seeking refuge from all the surrounding concrete. The Fundação Oscar e Maria Luisa Americano has a small forest and a museum. The Parque do Estado (also called the Parque do Ipiranga) surrounds the Museu do Ipiranga and has a beautiful garden.

SIDE TRIPS

São Paulo State is full of natural attractions and towns with artistic and historical treasures. Embu is famous for its furniture stores, and artisans from throughout Brazil sell their wares at its enormous weekend street fair. The healing waters beckon from the spas of Águas de São Pedro. You can go white-water rafting or hike past more than 17 waterfalls around Brotas. In Campos do Jordão you can imagine yourself at a European mountain retreat. On the island called Ilhabela, you can bask on a beautiful beach and swim, snorkel, or dive.

PORTRAITS

BRAZIL'S MELTING POT

São Paulo is a microcosm of Brazil's melting pot. To be Brazilian means to share a heritage that's Native American, Portuguese, and African. The mix is further seasoned with offspring of settlers from other parts of Europe, from Asia, or from the Middle East.

Most of the indigenous peoples encountered by the first Portuguese were members of the Tupi-Guarani language group

(2 of an estimated 180 languages spoken by roughly 200 tribes) and were nomadic hunter-gatherers who lived along the coast. Many Brazilian words and place names, such as Copacabana, are are words from those languages. Indeed, the country's name comes from *pau-brasil*, the indigenous term for the brazilwood tree (it was used to make a coveted red dye and was the nation's first major export).

The Africans brought to Brazil as slaves were primarily Yoruban (from what are today Liberia, Nigeria, Benin, and parts of Sudan) and Bantu (from Angola, Mozambique, and Zaire). These groups blended their spiritualistic and animist beliefs with the Roman Catholic traditions of their Portuguese masters. Cults arose that likened African gods and goddesses to Catholic saints, creating a completely new pantheon of *orixás* (deities); some groups adopted beliefs of the indigenous peoples as well. Although 70% of Brazilians are Roman Catholic, many are also members of such thriving cults as Candomblé (from Salvador), Macumba (from Rio de Janeiro), and Xangô (from Recife), to name a few. Those who aren't members are at least respectful of the cults and their traditions (politicians have even been known to court cult leaders). The nation's food and music were also strongly influenced by the Afro-Brazilians. And "samba" is an African word as well as an African rhythm.

When Napoléon invaded Portugal, King João VI and the royal family fled to Brazil. The marriage of his son, Dom Pedro, to the Austrian archduchess Leopoldina saw the advent of immigration by German-speaking colonists. Many put down roots in the south, where the climate was similar to that of their homelands. Today, there are southern communities filled with Bavarian-style architecture. After the American Civil War, some U.S. Southerners moved to Brazil; like the Germans, many settled in Brazil's south, though others chose the Amazon.

When Brazil abolished slavery in 1888, the nation actively recruited European agricultural laborers—Germans, Italians,

Spaniards, and Portuguese came to work the fields. They were followed by groups from Eastern Europe, Russia, and the Middle East. In 1908, 640 Japanese immigrants arrived in Brazil; by 1969, more than 200,000 of their countrymen had followed. Most settled in São Paulo and its environs, and most worked in agriculture. Today the city has the largest Japanese community outside Japan. It also has many more varieties of fruits and vegetables than it would have had if the Japanese had not been so successful.

OS BANDEIRANTES

In the 16th and 17th centuries, groups called *bandeiras* (literally "flags"; it's an archaic term for an assault force) set out on expeditions from São Paulo. Although the *bandeirantes* (bandeira members) are remembered as heroes, their objectives were far from noble. Their initial goal was to enslave Native Americans. Later, they were hired to capture escaped African slaves and destroy *quilombos*, communities these slaves created deep in the interior. Still, by heading inland at a time when most colonies were close to the shore, the bandeirantes inadvertently did Brazil a great service.

A fierce breed, they often adopted indigenous customs and voyaged for years at a time. Some went as far as the Amazon River; others only to what is today Minas Gerais, where gold was discovered; still others found deposits of precious gems. In their travels, they ignored the 1494 Treaty of Tordesillas, which established a boundary between Spanish and Portuguese lands. (The boundary was a vague north–south line roughly 1,600 km/1,000 mi west of the Cape Verde islands; the Portuguese were to control all lands—discovered and yet to be discovered—east of this line and the Spanish all lands to the west of it.) Other Brazilians followed the bandeirantes, and towns were founded, often in what was technically Spanish territory. These colonists eventually claimed full possession of the lands they settled, and thus Brazil's borders were greatly expanded.

Your checklist for a perfect journey

WAY AHEAD
- Devise a trip budget.
- Write down the five things you want most from this trip. Keep this list handy before and during your trip.
- Make plane or train reservations. Book lodging and rental cars.
- Arrange for pet care.
- Check your passport. Apply for a new one if necessary.
- Photocopy important documents and store in a safe place.

A MONTH BEFORE
- Make restaurant reservations and buy theater and concert tickets. Visit fodors.com for links to local events.
- Familiarize yourself with the local language or lingo.

TWO WEEKS BEFORE
- Replenish your supply of medications.
- Create your itinerary.
- Enjoy a book or movie set in your destination to get you in the mood.

- Develop a packing list. Shop for missing essentials. Repair and launder or dry-clean your clothes.

A WEEK BEFORE
- Stop newspaper deliveries. Pay bills.
- Acquire traveler's checks.
- Stock up on film.
- Label your luggage.
- Finalize your packing list— take less than you think you need.
- Create a toiletries kit filled with travel-size essentials.
- Get lots of sleep. Don't get sick before your trip.

A DAY BEFORE
- Drink plenty of water.
- Check your travel documents.
- Get packing!

DURING YOUR TRIP
- Keep a journal/scrapbook.
- Spend time with locals.
- Take time to explore. Don't plan too much.

In This Chapter

Updated by Karla Brunet

here and there

EACH NEIGHBORHOOD SEEMS A TESTAMENT to a different period of the city's history. The largely pedestrians-only hilltop and valley areas, particularly Vale do Anhangabaú, are where São Paulo's first inhabitants lived—Jesuit missionaries and treasure-hunting pioneers. Later these areas became Centro (downtown district), a financial and cultural center that's still home to the stock exchange and many banks. It's now the focus of revitalization efforts.

The Bela Vista and Bixiga (the city's little Italy) neighborhoods, near Centro, are home to many theaters and bars. In the 19th century, many families who made fortunes from coffee built whimsical mansions in the ridge-top Avenida Paulista neighborhood. Beginning with the post–World War II industrial boom, these homes gave way to skyscrapers. Many of the best hotels are also on or near this avenue.

During the economic growth of the 1970s, many businesses moved west, downhill to a former swamp. You'll find the tall buildings of Avenida Brigadeiro Faria Lima, the stylish homes of the Jardins neighborhood, and the Shopping Center Iguatemi (Brazil's first mall) just off the banks of the Rio Pinheiros. Large-scale construction of corporate headquarters continues south, between the Marginal Pinheiros Beltway and the Avenida Engenheiro Luís Carlos Berrini, not far from the luxurious Shopping Center Morumbi.

CENTRO

Even though the downtown district has its share of petty crime, it's one of the few places with a historical flavor. You can explore the areas where the city began and see examples of architecture, some of it beautifully restored, from the 19th century.

Numbers in the text correspond to numbers in the margin and on the São Paulo Centro map.

A Good Tour

The **EDIFÍCIO COPAN** ①, designed by Brazilian architect Oscar Niemeyer, seems an appropriate place to begin a tour. Farther up Avenida Ipiranga is the city's tallest building, the **EDIFÍCIO ITÁLIA** ② (you might want to return at the end of the day for a terrific view of the city from the bar or the restaurant on the 41st floor). Continue north along the avenue to the **PRAÇA DA REPÚBLICA** ③. Cross Ipiranga and walk down the pedestrians-only Rua Barão de Itapetininga, with its many shops and street vendors. Follow it to the neobaroque **TEATRO MUNICIPAL** ④, in the Praça Ramos de Azevedo. Head east across the square to the Viaduto do Chá, a monumental overpass above the Vale do Anhangabaú—the heart of São Paulo. At the end of this viaduct, turn right onto Rua Líbero Badaró and follow it to the baroque **IGREJA DE SÃO FRANCISCO DE ASSIS** ⑤. A short walk along Rua Benjamin Constant will bring you to the **PRAÇA DA SÉ** ⑥, the city's true center and the site of the Catedral Metropolitana da Sé.

You can take the metrô (subway) from the station at the cathedral west to the Barra Funda station and the **MEMORIAL DA AMÉRICA LATINA**. Or you can head north out of Praça da Sé and follow Rua Roberto Simonsen to the **SOLAR DA MARQUESA DE SANTOS** ⑦, the city's only surviving late-18th-century residence. Nearby is the **PÁTIO DO COLÉGIO** ⑧. Walk north along Rua Boa Vista; turn left onto Rua Anchieta and then left onto Rua 15 de Novembro. Number 275, on the left, houses

BOVESPA⑨, the São Paulo Stock Exchange. Near the end of Rua 15 de Novembro, at Rua João Brícola 24, stands the 36-floor **EDIFÍCIO BANESPA**⑩. To the northwest is the **EDIFÍCIO MARTINELLI**⑪. Walk two blocks up on Rua São Bento to the **BASÍLICA DE SÃO BENTO**⑫, a church constructed at the beginning of the 20th century. Near it is Café Girondino, a good spot for a break. From the basilica, you can take a train north from the São Bento station to the Luz stop and the **PINACOTECA DO ESTADO**⑬, the state gallery. On Avenida Tiradentes walk north to see the religious art at **MUSEU DE ARTE SACRA**⑭.

TIMING AND PRECAUTIONS

This route requires at least five hours on foot and use of the metrô, which is safe and clean. An early start will allow you to be more leisurely should one sight pique your interest more than another. If you're planning to take taxis or hire a driver, bear in mind that traffic jams are common.

Being a tourist in Centro is a bit hazardous. If you keep a low profile, and speak at least some Spanish (if not Portuguese), you'll most likely avoid being the target of thieves. Otherwise you might feel more comfortable touring with a guide. Whatever you do, leave your Rolex back at the hotel.

Sights to See

⑫ **BASÍLICA DE SÃO BENTO.** This church, constructed between 1910 and 1922, was designed by German architect Richard Berndl. Its enormous organ has some 6,000 pipes. *Largo de São Bento, tel. 011/228–3633. Free. Mon., Wed., and Fri. 5–1 and 2–7:45, Thurs. 2–7:45, Sat. 6–1 and 3–7:30, Sun. 5–1 and 3–6. Metrô: São Bento.*

⑨ **BOVESPA.** If you leave an ID with the guard at the front desk, you can go up to the mezzanine and watch the hurly-burly of the busy São Paulo Stock Exchange—a hub for the foreign investment Brazil has attracted in its efforts to privatize state-owned companies. Computer terminals in the observation gallery carry the latest stock quotes as well as general information in various

são paulo centro

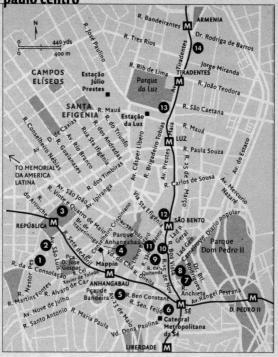

languages. BOVESPA offers tours in English, but only to representatives of foreign investment institutions. (If you fit this description, you can make arrangements in advance by faxing the Superintendência Executiva de Desenvolvimento at fax 011/239–4981.) *Rua 15 de Novembro 275, tel. 011/233–2000, Ext. 2456. Free. Weekdays 9–noon and 2–6. Metrô: São Bento.*

NEED A **CAFÉ GIRONDINO** is frequented by BOVESPA traders from
BREAK? happy hour until midnight. The bar serves good draft beer and sandwiches. Pictures on the wall depict Centro in its early days. *Rua Boa Vista 365, tel. 011/229–4574. Metrô: São Bento.*

⑩ EDIFÍCIO BANESPA. This structure offers a no-frills chance for a panoramic look at the city if you can't fit tea or drinks at the top of the Edifício Itália into your Centro tour. The 36-floor BANESPA Building was constructed in 1947 and modeled after New York's Empire State Building. A radio traffic reporter squints through the smog every morning from here. *Praça Antônio Prado, no phone. Free. Weekdays 9–6. Metrô: São Bento.*

❶ EDIFÍCIO COPAN. The architect of this serpentine apartment and office block, Oscar Niemeyer, went on to design much of Brasília, the nation's capital. The building has the clean, white, undulating curves characteristic of his work. Although many Brazilians prefer colonial architecture, all take pride in Niemeyer's international reputation. The Copan was constructed in 1950, and its 1,850 apartments house about 4,500 people. If you want to shop in the first-floor stores, be sure to do so before dark, when the area is overrun by prostitutes and transvestites. *Av. Ipiranga at Av. Consolação, no phone. Metrô: Anhangabaú.*

★ ❷ EDIFÍCIO ITÁLIA. To see the astounding view from atop the Itália Building, you'll have to patronize the bar or dining room of the Terraço Itália restaurant, on the 41st floor. As the restaurant is expensive (and isn't one of the city's best), afternoon tea or a drink is the quickest, least expensive option. Tea is served 3–5:30, and the bar opens at 6. *Av. Ipiranga 336, tel. 011/257–6566 (restaurant). Metrô: Anhangabaú.*

11 **EDIFÍCIO MARTINELLI.** Note the whimsical penthouse atop the Martinelli Building, the city's first skyscraper, which was built in 1929 by Italian immigrant-turned-count Giuseppe Martinelli. The rooftop is open weekdays 10:30–4. To get there, you need to get permission from the building manager on the ground floor and leave a photo ID at the front desk. Then take the elevator to the 34th floor and walk up two more flights. *Av. São João 35, no phone. Free. Metrô: São Bento.*

5 **IGREJA DE SÃO FRANCISCO DE ASSIS.** The baroque St. Francis of Assisi Church is actually two churches with a common name, one run by Catholic clergy and the other by lay brothers. One of the city's best-preserved Portuguese colonial buildings, it was built from 1647 to 1790. *Largo São Francisco 133, tel. 011/606–0081. Free. Daily 7 AM–8 PM; lay brothers' church weekdays 7–11:30 and 1–8, weekends 7 AM–10 AM. Metrô: Sé or Anhangabaú.*

OFF THE BEATEN PATH **MEMORIAL DA AMÉRICA LATINA** – A group of buildings designed by Oscar Niemeyer, the Latin American Memorial includes the Pavilhão da Criatividade Popular (Popular Creativity Pavilion), which has a permanent exhibition of Latin American handicrafts, and a model showing all the countries in Latin America. The Salão de Atos Building shows the panel *Tiradentes*, about an independence hero from Minas Gerais, painted by Cândido Portinari in 1949 and installed in 1989. *Av. Auro Soares de Moura Andrade 664, tel. 011/3823–9611, www. memorial.org.br. Free. Tues.–Sun. 9–6. Metrô: Barra Funda.*

14 **MUSEU DE ARTE SACRA.** If you can't get to Bahia during your stay in Brazil, the Museum of Sacred Art is a must-see. It houses an extremely interesting collection of wooden and terra-cotta masks, jewelry, and liturgical objects that date from the 17th century to the present. Don't miss the on-site convent, founded in 1774. Av. Tiradentes 676, tel. 011/3326–1373. R$4. Tues.–Fri. 11–6, weekends 10–7. Metrô: Luz.

8 **PÁTIO DO COLÉGIO.** São Paulo was founded by the Jesuits José de Anchieta and Manoel da Nóbrega in the College Courtyard in 1554. The church was constructed in 1896 in the same style as the chapel built by the Jesuits. *Pátio do Colégio 84, tel. 011/3105–6899. Church: Mon.–Sat. 8:15 AM–midnight, Sun. mass at 10 AM. Metrô: Sé.*

13 **PINACOTECA DO ESTADO.** The building that houses the State Art Gallery was constructed in 1905 and renovated in 1998. In the permanent collection you can see the work of such famous Brazilian artists as Tarsila do Amaral (whose work consists of colorful, somewhat abstract portraits), Anita Malfatti (a painter influenced by fauvism and German expressionism), Cândido Portinari (whose oil paintings have social and historical themes), Emiliano Di Cavalcanti (a multimedia artist whose illustrations, oil paintings, and engravings are influenced by cubism and contain Afro-Brazilian and urban themes), and Lasar Segall (an expressionist painter). *Praça da Luz 2, tel. 011/229–9844, www.uol.com.br/pinasp. R$5. Tues.–Sun. 10–6. Metrô: Luz.*

3 **PRAÇA DA REPÚBLICA.** Republic Square is the site of a huge Sunday street fair with arts and crafts, semiprecious stones, food, and often live music. Some artisans display their work all week long, so it's worth a peek anytime. *Metrô: República.*

6 **PRAÇA DA SÉ.** Two major metrô lines cross under the large, busy Cathedral Square. Migrants from Brazil's poor northeast often gather to enjoy their music and to sell and buy such regional items as medicinal herbs. It's also the central hangout for street children, and the focus of periodic (and controversial) police sweeps to get them off the street. The square, and most of the historic area and financial district to its north, have been set aside for pedestrians, official vehicles, and public transportation only.

7 **SOLAR DA MARQUESA DE SANTOS.** This 18th-century manor house was bought by Marquesa de Santos in 1843. It now contains a museum that hosts temporary exhibitions. *Rua Roberto Simonsen 136, tel. 011/3106–2218. Free. Tues.–Sun. 9–5. Metrô: Sé.*

④ **TEATRO MUNICIPAL.** Inspired by the Paris Opéra, the Municipal Theater was built between 1903 and 1911 with art nouveau elements. *Hamlet* was the first play presented, and the house went on to host such luminaries as Isadora Duncan in 1916 and Anna Pavlova in 1919. Unfortunately, the fully restored auditorium, resplendent with gold leaf, moss-green velvet, marble, and mirrors, is open only to those attending cultural events, but sometimes you can walk in for a quick look at the vestibule. *Praça Ramos de Azevedo, tel. 011/223–3022. Metrô: Anhangabaú.*

LIBERDADE

At the beginning of the 20th century, large groups of Japanese arrived to work as contract farm laborers in São Paulo State. During the next five decades, thousands more followed, forming what is now the largest Japanese colony outside Japan. Distinguished today by a large number of college graduates and successful businesspeople, professionals, and politicians, the colony has made important contributions to Brazilian agriculture and the seafood industry. The Liberdade neighborhood, which is south of Praça da Sé behind the cathedral and whose entrance is marked by a series of red porticoes, is home to many first-, second-, and third-generation Nippo-Brazilians. Clustered around Avenida Liberdade, you'll find shops with everything from imported bubble gum to miniature robots to Kabuki face paint. The Sunday street fair holds many surprises.

Numbers in the text correspond to numbers in the margin and on the São Paulo City map.

A Good Tour

From the **PRAÇA LIBERDADE** ⑮, by the Liberdade metrô station, walk south along Rua Galvão Bueno. About six blocks from the square is the intriguing **MUSEU DA IMIGRAÇÃO JAPONESA** ⑯.

TIMING AND PRECAUTIONS

The best time to visit Liberdade is on Sunday during the street fair, when you'll find tents that sell Asian food, crafts, and souvenirs. This tour takes about two hours—a little longer if you linger in the museum. Don't take this tour at night.

Sights to See

⑯ **MUSEU DA IMIGRAÇÃO JAPONESA.** The Museum of Japanese Immigration has two floors of exhibits about Nippo-Brazilian culture and farm life and Japanese contributions to Brazilian horticulture. (They're credited with introducing the persimmon, the azalea, the tangerine, and the kiwi to Brazil, among other things.) Call ahead to arrange for an English-language tour. *Rua São Joaquim 381, tel. 011/279–5465. R$3. Tues.–Sun. 1:30–5:30. Metrô: São Joaquim.*

⑮ **PRAÇA LIBERDADE.** On Sunday morning Liberdade hosts a sprawling Asian food and crafts fair, where the free and easy Brazilian ethnic mix is in plain view; you may see, for example, Afro-Brazilians dressed in colorful kimonos hawking grilled shrimp on a stick. Liberdade also hosts several ethnic celebrations, such as April's Hanamatsuri, commemorating the birth of the Buddha. *Metrô: Liberdade.*

AVENIDA PAULISTA AND BIXIGA

Money once poured into and out of the coffee barons' mansions that lined Avenida Paulista, making it, in a sense, the financial hub. And so it is today, though instead of mansions you'll find many major banks. Like the barons before them, many of these financial institutions generously support the arts. Numerous places have changing exhibitions—often free—in the Paulista neighborhood. Nearby Bixiga, São Paulo's Little Italy, is full of restaurants.

são paulo city

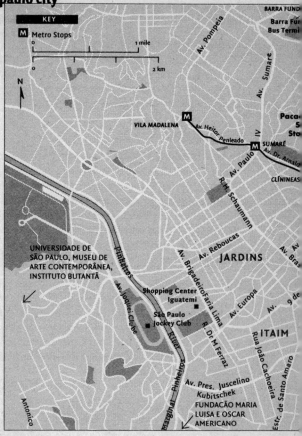

KEY

M Metro Stops

0   1 mile

0   2 km

N

BARRA FUND

Barra Fú
Bus Termi

Av. Pompeia

Av. Sumaré

Av. Sumaré

Paca
S
Sto

VILA MADALENA   Av. Heitor Penleado

M IV

M SUMARÉ

Av. Dr. Arnald

Av. Paulo

CLÍNINEAS

R. H. Schaumann

Av. Reboucas

Av. Bras

JARDINS

Av. Brigadeiro Faria Lima

Av. 9 de

UNIVERSIDADE DE
SÃO PAULO, MUSEU DE
ARTE CONTEMPORÂNEA,
INSTITUTO BUTANTÃ

Shopping Center
Iguatemi

Av. Europa

São Paulo
Jockey Club

R. Dr M. Ferraz

Av. Joquei Clube

ITAIM

Rua João Cachoeira

Marginal Pinheiros

Antonico

Av. Pres. Juscelino
Kubitschek

FUNDACÃO MARIA
LUISA E OSCAR
AMERICANO

Estr. de Santo Amaro

Marginal Pinheiros

Casa das
Rosas, 22

Centro Cultural
FIESP, 19

Espaço Cultural
Citibank, 20

Instituto Cultural
Itaú, 21

Museu de
Arte Moderna
(MAM), 26

Museu de
Arte de São Paulo
(MASP), 17

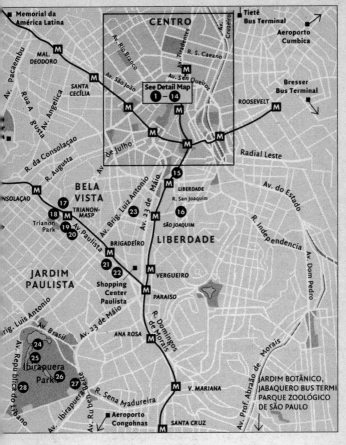

Museu da
Imigração
Japonesa, 16

Museu Memória
do Bixiga, 23

Parque Trianon, 18

Pavilhão da
Bienal, 27

Pavilhão
Japonês, 25

Planetário, 24

Praça
Liberdade, 15

Viveiro
Manequinho
Lopes, 28

A Good Tour

Begin your tour at the **MUSEU DE ARTE DE SÃO PAULO (MASP)** ⑰, which has Brazil's best collection of fine art. Across the street is **PARQUE TRIANON** ⑱, where many businesspeople eat lunch. Leaving the park, veer right onto Avenida Paulista and head for the **CENTRO CULTURAL FIESP** ⑲, which frequently has art and theatrical presentations. Farther down Paulista is the **ESPAÇO CULTURAL CITIBANK** ⑳, a gallery with temporary exhibitions. Continue a few more blocks along Paulista to the **INSTITUTO CULTURAL ITAÚ** ㉑, a great place to see contemporary Brazilian art. In the next block is the **CASA DAS ROSAS** ㉒, with yet another noteworthy gallery. From here you can hop a bus or a taxi to the **MUSEU MEMÓRIA DO BIXIGA** ㉓, with its displays on Italian immigration.

TIMING AND PRECAUTIONS

This tour takes about five hours, including a visit to MASP and the Museu do Bixiga. Busy, well-lighted Avenida Paulista may well be the safest place in city. Even so, stay alert and hold onto your bags, particularly in Parque Trianon.

Sights to See

㉒ **CASA DAS ROSAS.** The House of the Roses, a French-style mansion, seems out of place next to the skyscrapers of Paulista. It was built in 1935 by famous paulistano architect Ramos de Azevedo for one of his daughters. The building was home to the same family until 1986, when it was made an official municipal landmark. It was opened as a cultural center—with changing fine-arts exhibitions and multimedia displays by up-and-coming artists—in 1991, and it's one of the avenue's few remaining early 20th-century buildings. *Av. Paulista 37, Paraíso, tel. 011/251–5271, www.dialdata.com.br/casadasrosas. Free. Tues.–Sun. 2–8. Metrô: Brigadeiro.*

⑲ **CENTRO CULTURAL FIESP.** The cultural center of São Paulo State's Federation of Industry has a theater, a library of art books, and temporary art exhibits. *Av. Paulista 1313, Jardim Paulista, tel. 011/253–5877. Free. Tues.–Sun. 9–7. Metrô: Trianon.*

20 ESPAÇO CULTURAL CITIBANK. Citibank's cultural space hosts temporary exhibitions of Brazilian art. *Av. Paulista 1111, Jardim Paulista, tel. 011/5576–2744. Free. Weekdays 9–7, weekends 10–5. Metrô: Trianon.*

21 INSTITUTO CULTURAL ITAÚ. Maintained by Itaú, one of Brazil's largest private banks, this cultural institute has art shows as well as lectures, workshops, and films. Its library specializes in works on Brazilian art and culture. *Av. Paulista 149, Paraíso, tel. 011/238–1700, www.itaucultural.org.br. Free. Tues.–Sun. 10–7. Metrô: Brigadeiro.*

NEED A
BREAK?
Before heading to the Museu Memória do Bixiga, try a *baurú* at **PONTO CHIC** (Praça Osvaldo Cruz 26, Bixiga, tel. 011/289–1480)—a block east of Instituto Cultural Itaú, across Avenida Paulista. The restaurant claims to have invented this sandwich, which is made with roast beef, tomato, cucumber, and steam-heated mozzarella.

★ **17 MUSEU DE ARTE DE SÃO PAULO (MASP).** A striking low-rise elevated on two massive concrete pillars 77 m (256 ft) apart, the São Paulo Museum of Art contains the city's premier collection of fine arts. Highlights include dazzling works by Hieronymous Bosch, Vincent van Gogh, Pierre-Auguste Renoir, and Edgar Degas. Lasar Segall and Cândido Portinari are two of the many Brazilian artists represented in the collection. The huge open area beneath the museum is often used for cultural events and is the site of a Sunday antiques fair. *Av. Paulista 1578, Bela Vista, tel. 011/251–5644, www2.uol.com.br/masp. R$10. Tues.–Sun. 11–6. Metrô: Trianon.*

23 MUSEU MEMÓRIA DO BIXIGA. This museum, established in 1980, contains objects that belonged to Italian immigrants who lived in the Bixiga neighborhood. On weekends you can extend your tour to include the **Feira do Bixiga,** at Praça Dom Orione, where handicrafts, antiques, and furniture are sold. *Rua dos Ingleses 118, Bixiga, tel. 011/285–5009. Free. Wed.–Sun. 2–5.*

⑱ PARQUE TRIANON. The park was originally created in 1892 as a showcase for local vegetation. In 1968, Roberto Burle Marx (the Brazilian landscaper famed for Rio's mosaic-tile beachfront sidewalks) renovated it and incorporated new trees. You can escape the noise of the street and admire the flora while seated on óne of the benches sculpted to look like chairs. *Rua Peixoto Gomide 949, Jardim Paulista, tel. 011/289–2160. Free. Daily 6–6. Metrô: Trianon.*

PARQUE IBIRAPUERA

Only 15 minutes by taxi from downtown, Ibirapuera is São Paulo's answer to New York's Central Park, although it's slightly less than half the size and gets infinitely more crowded on sunny weekends. In the 1950s the land, which originally contained the municipal nurseries, was chosen as the site of a public park to commemorate the city's 400th anniversary. Oscar Niemeyer was called in to head the team of architects assigned to the project. The park was inaugurated in 1954, and some pavilions used for the opening festivities still sit amid its 395 acres. You'll also find jogging and biking paths, a lake, and rolling lawns.

A Good Walk

Enter at Gate 9 and walk around the lake to the starry sights at the **PLANETÁRIO** ㉔. As you exit the planetarium, veer left to the **PAVILHÃO JAPONÊS** ㉕. Then turn left and follow the path to the Marquise do Ibirapuera, a structure that connects several buildings, including the **MUSEU DE ARTE MODERNA (MAM)** ㉖ and the **PAVILHÃO DA BIENAL** ㉗, which houses the park branch of the Museu de Arte Contemporânea. When you exit the compound, walk toward Gate 7 and the **VIVEIRO MANEQUINHO LOPES** ㉘, with its many species of Brazilian trees.

TIMING AND PRECAUTIONS

The park deserves a whole day, though you can probably do this tour in one afternoon. Avoid the park on Sunday, when it gets really crowded, and after sundown.

Sights to See

26 MUSEU DE ARTE MODERNA (MAM). The permanent collection of the Museum of Modern Art includes more than 2,600 paintings, sculptures (some in a sculpture garden out front), and drawings from the Brazilian modernist movement, which began in the 1920s, when artists were developing a new form of expression influenced by the city's rapid industrial growth. The museum also hosts temporary exhibits that feature works by new local artists and has a library with more than 20,000 books, photographs, videotapes, and CD-ROMs. In a 1982 renovation, Brazilian architect Lina Bo Bardi gave the building a wall of glass, creating a giant window that beckons you to peek at what's inside. *Gate 10, tel. 011/5549–9688. R$5 (free on Tues.). Tues., Wed., Fri. noon–6, Thurs. noon–10, weekends and holidays 10–6.*

NEED A BREAK? The **BAR DO MAM**, inside the Museu de Arte Moderna, has sandwiches, pies, soda, coffee, and tea. The comfortable chairs enable you to thoroughly rest.

27 PAVILHÃO DA BIENAL. From October through November in every even-numbered year, this pavilion hosts the Bienal (Biennial) art exhibition, which draws more than 250 artists from more than 60 countries. The first such event was held in 1951 in Parque Trianon and drew artists from 21 countries. It was moved to this Oscar Niemeyer–designed building—with its large open spaces and floors connected by circular slopes—after Ibirapuera Park's 1954 inauguration. The pavilion also houses a branch of the **Museu de Arte Contemporânea** (MAC; Museum of Contemporary Art), whose main branch is at the Universidade de São Paulo. Exhibits are created from the museum's collection of works by such European artists as Pablo Picasso, Amedeo Modigliani, Wassily Kandinsky, Joan Miró, and Henri Matisse. Look also for the works of Brazilian artists such as Anita Malfatti, Tarsila do Amaral, Cândido Portinari, and Emiliano Di Cavalcanti. *Gate 10, tel. 011/5573–9932, www.mac.usp.br. Free. Museum: Tues.–Sun. noon–6.*

㉕ PAVILHÃO JAPONÊS. An exact replica of the Katsura Imperial Palace in Kyoto, Japan, the Japanese Pavilion is also one of the structures built for the park's inauguration. It was designed by University of Tokyo professor Sutemi Horiguti and built in Japan. It took four months to reassemble beside the man-made lake in the midst of the Japanese-style garden. In the main building you'll find displays of samurai clothes, 11th-century sculptures, and pottery and sculpture from several dynasties. Rooms used for traditional tea ceremonies are upstairs. *Gate 10, tel. 011/5573–6453. R$2. Weekends and holidays 10–5.*

㉔ PLANETÁRIO. Paulistanos love the planetarium and frequently fill the 350 seats under its 48-ft-high dome. You can see a projection of the 8,900 stars and five planets (Mercury, Venus, Mars, Jupiter, and Saturn) clearly visible in the southern hemisphere. Shows last 50 minutes and always depict the night sky just as it is on the evening of your visit. Be sure to buy tickets at least 15 minutes before the session. *Gate 10, Av. Pedro Álvares Cabral, tel. 011/5575–5206. R$5. Weekends and holidays, projections at 3:30 and 5:30.*

㉘ VIVEIRO MANEQUINHO LOPES. The Manequinho Lopes Nursery is where most plants and trees used by the city are grown. The original was built in the 1920s; the current version was designed by Roberto Burle Marx. You'll find specimens of such Brazilian trees as *ipê, pau-jacaré,* and *pau-brasil,* the tree after which the country was named (the red dye it produced was greatly valued by the Europeans). The Bosque da Leitura (Reading Forest) has a stand that provides books and magazines (all in Portuguese) as well as chairs so people can read among the trees. *Enter park from Av. República do Líbano, no phone. Daily 5–5.*

ELSEWHERE IN SÃO PAULO

Several far-flung sights are worth a taxi ride to see. West of Centro is the Universidade de São Paulo (USP), which has two very interesting museums: a branch of the Museu de Arte Contemporânea and the Instituto Butantã, with its collection of creatures that slither and crawl. Head southwest of Centro to the Fundação Maria Luisa e Oscar Americano, a museum with a forest and garden in the residential neighborhood of Morumbi. In the Parque do Estado, southeast of Centro, are the Jardim Botânico and the Parque Zoológico de São Paulo.

Sights to See

FUNDAÇÃO MARIA LUISA E OSCAR AMERICANO. A private wooded estate is the setting for the Maria Luisa and Oscar Americano Foundation. Exhibits feature objects from the Portuguese colonial and imperial periods as well as modern pieces. You'll find paintings, furniture, sacred art, silver, porcelain, engravings, personal possessions of the Brazilian royal family, tapestries, and sculpture. *Av. Morumbi 3700, Morumbi, tel. 011/3742–0077, www.fundacaooscaramericano.org.br. R$5. Tues.–Fri. 11–5, weekends 10–5.*

JARDIM BOTÂNICO. The Botanical Gardens contain about 3,000 plants belonging to more than 340 native species. You'll also find a greenhouse with Atlantic rain-forest species, an orchid house, and a collection of aquatic plants. *Av. Miguel Stéfano 3031, Parque do Estado, tel. 011/5584–6300. R$2. Wed.–Sun. 9–5.*

★ ☺ **PARQUE ZOOLÓGICO DE SÃO PAULO.** The 200-acre São Paulo Zoo has more than 3,000 animals, and many of its 410 species— such as the mico-leão-dourado (golden lion tamarin monkey)—are endangered. Its attractions include a lake with small islands, where monkeys live in houses on stilts, and the Casa do Sangue Frio (House of Cold Blood) with reptilian and amphibious creatures. *Av. Miguel Stéfano 4241, Parque do Estado, tel. 011/276–0811, www.zoologico.com.br. R$7. Tues.–Sun. 9–5.*

UNIVERSIDADE DE SÃO PAULO. Consider taking a stroll around the grounds of the country's largest university (founded in 1934) just to soak in the atmosphere of a Brazilian campus. Art lovers can also visit the university branch of the **Museu de Arte Contemporânea,** which consists of a main building and an annex, to see works by world-renowned contemporary European and Brazilian artists. *Main bldg.: Rua da Reitoria 109, Cidade Universitária, tel. 011/3818–3538, www.usp.br. Free. Tues.– Wed. and Fri. 10–7, Thurs. 11–8, weekends 10–4.*

In 1888 a Brazilian scientist, with the aid of the state government, turned a farmhouse into a center for the production of snake serum. Today the **Instituto Butantã** has more than 70,000 snakes, spiders, scorpions, and lizards. It still extracts venom and processes it into serum that's made available to victims of poisonous bites throughout Latin America. Unfortunately, the institute has suffered from underfunding; it's somewhat run-down, and its exhibits aren't as accessible to children as they could be. *Av. Vital Brasil 1500, Cidade Universitária, tel. 011/3813– 7222. R$1.5. Tues.–Sun. 9–4:30.*

BEACHES

São Paulo rests on a plateau 72 km (46 mi) inland. If you can avoid traffic, getaways are fairly quick on the parallel Imigrantes (BR 160) or Anchieta (BR 150) highways, each of which becomes one-way on weekends and holidays. Although the port of Santos (near the Cubatão Industrial Park) has *praias* (beaches) in and around it, the cleanest and best beaches are along what is known as the North Shore. Mountains and bits of Atlantic rain forest hug numerous small, sandy coves. On weekdays when school is in session, the beaches are gloriously deserted.

Buses run along the coast from São Paulo's Jabaquara terminal, near the Congonhas Airport, and there are once-daily trains from the Estação da Luz to Santos and the sands along the North Shore. Beaches often don't have bathrooms or phones right on the sands, nor do they have beach umbrellas or chairs for rent.

They generally do have restaurants nearby, however, or at least vendors selling sandwiches, soft drinks, and beer.

BARRA DO SAHY. Families with young children favor this small, quiet beach 165 km (102 mi) north of the city on the Rio–Santos Highway. Its narrow strip of sand (with a bay and a river on one side and rocks on the other) is steep but smooth, and the water is clean and very calm. Kayakers paddle about and divers are drawn to the nearby Ilha das Couves. Area restaurants serve only basic fish dishes with rice and salad. Note that Barra do Sahy's entrance is atop a slope and appears suddenly—be on the lookout.

CAMBURI. The young and the restless flock here to sunbathe, surf, and party. At the center of the beach is a cluster of cafés, ice-cream shops, bars, and the Tiê restaurant. The service may be slow, but Tiê's menu is extensive, and the open-air setup is divine. Another good bet is Bom Dia Vietnã, with its delicious pizzas, sandwiches, sushi, salads, and banana pie. Camburi is just north of Barra do Sahy. If you're coming from the south, use the second entrance; although it's unpaved, it's in better shape than the first entrance.

MARESIAS. Some of the North Shore's most beautiful houses line the Rio–Santos road (SP 055) on the approach to Maresias. The beach itself is also nice, with its 4-km (2-mi) stretch of white sand and its clean, green waters that are good swimming and surfing. Maresias is popular with a young crowd.

UBATUBA. Many of the more than 30 beaches around Ubatuba are truly beautiful enough to merit the 229-km (148-mi) drive north along the Carvalho Pinto and Oswaldo Cruz highways. For isolation and peace, try Prumirim Beach, which can only be reached by boat; for a little more action try the centrally located Praia Grande, with its many kiosks. Ubatuba itself has a very active nightlife. In nearby Itaguá you'll find several gift shops, a branch of the Projeto Tartarugas Marinhas (Marine Turtles Project), and a large aquarium.

In This Chapter

Updated by Karla Brunet

eating out

SÃO PAULO'S SOCIAL LIFE CENTERS ON DINING OUT, and there are a great many establishments from which to choose (new ones seem to open as often as the sun rises), particularly in the Jardins district. You'll find German, Japanese, Spanish, Italian, and Portuguese restaurants as well as top-quality French and Indian spots. There are innumerable *churrascarias* (places that serve a seemingly endless stream of barbecued meat), which are beloved by paulistanos. As in other Brazilian cities, many restaurants serve feijoada on Wednesday and Saturday; top restaurants do it up in fancy buffets.

PRICES AND DRESS

São Paulo restaurants frequently change their credit-card policies, sometimes adding a surcharge for their use or not accepting them at all. Though most places don't generally require jacket and tie, people tend to dress up; establishments in the $$ to $$$$ categories expect you to look neat and elegant. You might feel uncomfortable in jeans.

CATEGORY	COST*
$$$$	*over R$40*
$$$	*R$30–$40*
$$	*R$20–R$30*
$	*R$10–R$20*
¢	*under R$10*

*per person for a dinner entrée

BRAZILIAN

$$$–$$$$ **BARGAÇO.** The original Bargaço has long been considered the best Bahian restaurant in Salvador. If you can't make it to the northeast, be sure to have a meal in the São Paulo branch. Seafood is the calling card. *Rua Oscar Freire 1189, Cerqueira César, tel. 011/3085–5058. AE, DC, MC, V. Metrô: Consolação.*

$$$ **BABY BEEF RUBAIYAT.** Galician Belarmino Iglesias was once an employee at this restaurant; today he owns it, and he and his son run it. The meat they serve is from their ranch in Mato Grosso do Sul State. The buffet features charcoal-grilled fare—from baby boar (on request at least two hours in advance) and steak to chicken and salmon—and a salad bar with all sorts of options. Wednesday and Saturday see a feijoada; on Friday the emphasis is on seafood. *Alameda Santos 86, Paraíso, tel. 011/289–6366. V. No dinner Sun. Metrô: Paraíso.*

$$$ **DONA LUCINHA.** Mineiro dishes—from the Minas Gerais State— are the specialties at this modest eatery with plain wooden tables. The classic cuisine is served as a buffet only: more than 50 stone pots hold dishes like *feijão tropeiro* (beans with manioc flour). Save room for a dessert of ambrosia. *Av. Chibaras 399, Moema, tel. 011/5549–2050; Rua Bela Cintra 2325, Jardins, tel. 011/3062–1973. AE, DC, MC, V.*

$$–$$$$ **ESPLANADA GRILL.** The beautiful people hang out in the bar of
★ this highly regarded churrascaria. The thinly sliced *picanha* steak (similar to rump steak) is excellent; it goes well with a house salad (hearts of palm and shredded, fried potatoes), onion rings, and creamed spinach. The restaurant's rendition of the traditional *pão de queijo* (cheese bread) is just right. *Rua Haddock Lobo 1682, Jardins, tel. 011/3081–3199. V.*

$$–$$$ **CONSULADO MINEIRO.** During and after the Saturday crafts and antiques fair in Praça Benedito Calixto, it may take an hour to get a table at this homey restaurant set in a house. Among the traditional mineiro dishes are the mandioca com carne de sol (cassava with salted meat) appetizer and the tutu (pork loin with beans, pasta, cabbage, and rice) entrée. Rua Praça Benedito Calixto 74, Pinheiros, tel. 011/3064–3882. AE, DC, MC, V. Closed Mon.

$–$$ SUJINHO–BISTECA D'OURO. The modest Sujinho serves churrasco without any frills. It's the perfect place for those who simply want to eat an honest, gorgeous piece of meat. Rua da Consolação 2078, Cerqueira César, tel. 011/231–5207. No credit cards. Metrô: Consolação.

¢–$ FREVO. Paulistanos of all ilks and ages flock to this Jardins luncheonette for its beirute sandwiches, draft beer, and fruit juices in flavors such as acerola (Antilles cherry), passion fruit, and papaya. Rua Oscar Freire 603, Jardins, tel. 011/3082–3434. No credit cards.

CONTINENTAL

$$–$$$$ PADDOCK. Both locations of this restaurant are considered ideal spots for relaxed business lunches; neither is open on weekends. Men and women of affairs eat and chat in comfortable armchairs. The Continental cuisine is prepared with finesse; try the lamb with mint sauce or the poached haddock. Av. São Luís 258, Centro, tel. 011/257–4768. Metrô: Anhangabaú or República; Av. Brigadeiro Faria Lima 1912, Loja 110, Jardim Paulistano, tel. 011/3814–3582. AE, DC, MC, V. Closed weekends.

$–$$$$ CANTALOUP. That paulistanos take food seriously has not been lost on the folks at Cantaloup. The two dining areas are in a converted warehouse. Oversize photos decorate the walls of the slightly formal room, and a fountain and plants make the second area feel more casual. Try the filet mignon with risotto or the St. Peter's fillet with almonds and spinach. Save room for the papaya ice cream with mango soup or the mango ice cream with papaya soup. Rua Manoel Guedes 474, Itaim Bibi, tel. 011/3846–6445. AE, DC, MC, V.

ECLECTIC

$$$–$$$$ **LA TAMBOUILLE.** This Italo-French restaurant with a partially enclosed garden isn't just a place to be seen; many believe it also has the best food in town. Among chef André Fernandes's recommended dishes are the linguini with fresh mussels and prawn sauce and the filet mignon *rosini* (served with foie gras and risotto with saffron). *Av. Nove de Julho 5925, Jardim Europa, tel. 011/ 3079–6276. AE, DC, MC, V.*

$$–$$$ **BAR DES ARTS.** A great place for lunch or drinks (it's a favorite with businesspeople), the Bar des Arts is set in a charming arcade near a flower shop, a wine shop, and a fountain. You'll find both a buffet and à la carte options at lunch. *Rua Pedro Humberto 9, at Rua Horacio Lafer, Itaim Bibi, tel. 011/3849–7828. AE, DC, MC, V. Closed Mon.*

$–$$$ ★ **MESTIÇO.** Tribal masks peer down at you from the walls of the large, modern dining room. Consider the Thai *huan-hin* (chicken with shiitake mushrooms in ginger sauce and rice) followed by a dessert of lemon ice cream with *baba de moça* (a syrup made with egg whites and sugar). *Rua Fernando de Albuquerque 277, Consolação, tel. 011/256–3165. AE, DC, MC, V. Metrô: Consolação.*

$–$$ **SPOT.** This place, the closest thing to a chic diner that you'll find, is just one door up from MASP. The salads and the pasta dishes are good bets; come early, though, as it gets crowded after 10 PM. *Alameda Rocha Azevedo 72, Cerqueira César, tel. 011/283–0946. AE, DC, MC, V. Metrô: Consolação.*

¢–$ **MILK & MELLOW.** Before or after a night of clubbing, stop for the great sandwiches, hamburgers, and milk shakes in a relaxed atmosphere. It's open weekdays until 4 AM and weekends until 6 AM. *Av. Cidade Jardim 1085, Itaim Bibi, tel. 011/3849–8916. MC, V.*

FRENCH

$$$$ **LE COQ HARDY.** This upscale restaurant has two chefs: one is a veteran of the top French kitchens in Brazil, and the other spent many years cooking in France. The grilled foie gras and mango, the escargots with mushrooms in an anise-and-wine sauce, and the roast duck are all highly recommended. *Rua Jerônimo da Veiga 461, Itaim Bibi, tel. 011/3079–3344. AE, DC, MC, V. Closed Sun.*

$$–$$$$ BISTRÔ JAÚ. The name of this place has recently changed (formerly Laurent) but not much else has. Chef Laurent Suadeau, famous for his use of Brazilian ingredients to create French nouvelle cuisine, runs the kitchen. Businesspeople from Avenida Paulista appreciate the fine decor and and the superb yet inexpensive (compared to dinner) lunch menu. *Alameda Jaú 1606, Jardins, tel. 011/3085–5573. AE, DC, MC, V.*

$$–$$$$ LA CASSEROLE. Facing a little Centro flower market, this charming bistro has been around for generations. Surrounded by wood-paneled walls decorated with eclectic posters, you can dine on such delights as *gigot d'agneau aux soissons* (roast leg of lamb in its own juices, served with white beans) and cherry strudel. *Largo do Arouche 346, Centro, tel. 011/220–6283. AE, DC, MC, V. Closed Mon. No lunch Sat.*

$$–$$$$ FREDDY. You'll leave behind the grunge and noise of the streets when you walk through the doors of this long-lived eatery with the feel of an upscale Parisian bistro. Try the duck with Madeira sauce and apple purée, the pheasant with herb sauce, or the hearty cassoulet (white beans, lamb, duck, and garlic sausage). *Praça Dom Gastão Liberal Pinto 111, Itaim Bibi, tel. 011/3849–0977. AE, DC, MC, V. No dinner Sun., no lunch Sat.*

$ LA TARTINE. This small restaurant has movie posters on its walls
★ and simple but comfortable furniture. The menu changes daily; a favorite is the classic coq au vin. *Rua Fernando de Albuquerque 267, Consolação, tel. 011/259–2090. V. Closed Sun.–Mon. Metrô: Consolação.*

INDIAN

$$–$$$$ GANESH. Many consider this the best Indian eatery in town. The traditional menu includes curries and *tandoori* dishes. The decor is all Indian artwork and tapestries. *Morumbi Shopping Center, Av. Roque Petroni Jr. 1089, Morumbi, tel. 011/5181–4748. AE, DC, MC, V.*

ITALIAN

$$$–$$$$ FASANO. A family-owned northern Italian classic, this restaurant is as famous for its superior cuisine as for its exorbitant prices. The new chef, Salvatore Loi, has added to the menu dishes like seafood ravioli with a white wine sauce. Despite the cost, the luxe decor—marble, mahogany, and mirrors—has seen better days. *Rua Haddock Lobo 1644, Jardins, tel. 011/3062–4000. AE, DC, MC, V. Closed Sun. No lunch.*

$$–$$$$ CA' D'ORO. This is a longtime northern Italian favorite among Brazilian bigwigs, many of whom have their own tables in the Old World–style dining room. Quail, osso buco, and veal-and-raisin ravioli are winners, but the specialty is the Piedmontese *gran bollito misto*, steamed meats and vegetables accompanied by three sauces and served from a cart. *Grande Hotel Ca' D'Oro, Rua Augusta 129, Bela Vista, tel. 011/236–4300. AE, DC, MC, V. Metrô: Anhangabaú.*

$$–$$$$ FAMIGLIA MANCINI. A huge provolone cheese is the first thing
★ you see at this warm, cheerful restaurant. An incredible buffet with cheeses, olives, sausages, and much more is the perfect place to find a tasty appetizer. The menu has many terrific pasta options, such as the cannelloni with palm hearts and a four-cheese sauce. *Rua Avanhandava 81, Centro, tel. 011/256–4320. AE, DC, MC, V. Metrô: Anhangabaú.*

$$–$$$$ LELLIS TRATTORIA. Photos of famous patrons (mostly Brazilian actors) hang on the walls, and the doors and bar are made of metal, giving this typical Italian cantina a sophisticated twist. Salmon fillet *marinatta* (in white sauce with potatoes, raisins, and rice) is the best choice on the menu. *Rua Bela Cintra 1849, Jardim Paulista, tel. 011/3064–2727. AE, DC, MC, V.*

$$–$$$$ LA VECCHIA CUCINA. Chef Sergio Arno changed the face of the city's Italian restaurants with his *nuova cucina*, exemplified by such dishes as frogs'-legs risotto and duck ravioli with watercress sauce. Well-to-do patrons feast either in the ocher-color dining room decorated with Italian engravings and fresh flowers or in the glassed-in garden gazebo. *Rua Pedroso Alvarenga 1088, Itaim Bibi, tel. 011/3167–2822. AE, DC, MC, V. No dinner Sun., no lunch Sat.*

$–$$$$ GIGETTO. The walls are adorned with theater posters, a tribute to the actors who dine here after performing. The modest decor is offset by the elaborate menu's more than 200 delicious options. Try the cappelletti *à romanesca* (with chopped ham, peas, mushrooms, and white cream sauce). *Rua Avanhandava 63, Centro, tel. 011/256–9804. AE, DC, MC, V. Metrô: Anhangabaú.*

$–$$$ ROPERTO. Plastic flowers adorn the walls at this typical Bixiga cantina. You won't be alone if you order the traditional and ever-popular fusilli *ao sugo* (with tomato sauce). *Rua 13 de Maio 634, Bixiga, tel. 011/288–2573. DC, MC, V.*

$–$$$ SANTO COLOMBA. This Italian restaurant near the Paulista hotels isn't inexpensive, but some say that for the money you won't find better food in the city. It was originally built in Rio de Janeiro's Jóque Clube (Jockey Club) before being brought lock, stock, and barrel (or rather wooden walls, French tiles, and carved wooden bar) to its current location. You can feast on pasta with shrimp, squid, tomato, and garlic while listening to live piano music. *Alameda Lorena 1165, Jardins, tel. 011/3061–3588. AE, DC, MC.*

$–$$ JARDIM DI NAPOLI. Just about everywhere you look in this restaurant you'll see the white, green, and red of the Italian flag. People come for the unmatchable *polpettone alla parmigiana*, a huge meatball with mozzarella and tomato sauce. There are also many other meat dishes, pasta selections, and pizza. *Rua Doutor Martinico Prado 463, Higienópolis, tel. 011/3666–3022. No credit cards.*

$ RITZ. An animated crowd chatters as contemporary pop music plays in the background. Although each day sees a different special, one of the most popular dishes is the *bife à milanesa* (a breaded beef cutlet) with creamed spinach and french fries.

são paulo dining

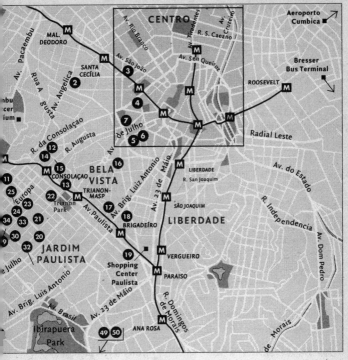

Alameda França 1088, Cerqueira César, tel. 011/3088–6808. AE, V. Metrô: Consolação.

$ MAMMA MIA. This buffet eatery is known for its grilled chicken, but you can also have salad and pasta here for R$15. *Av. Moema 41, Moema, tel. 011/5051–5100. AE, DC, MC, V.*

JAPANESE

$$$–$$$$ NAGAYAMA. Low-key, trustworthy, and well loved, both Nagayama locations consistently serve excellent sushi and sashimi. The chefs like to experiment: the California *uramaki* Philadelphia has rice, cream cheese, grilled salmon, roe, cucumber, and spring onions rolled together. *Rua Bandeira Paulista 369, Itaim Bibi, tel. 011/ 3079–7553; Rua da Consolação 3397, Cerqueira César, tel. 011/3064– 0110. AE, DC, MC.*

$$ KOMAZUSHI. Real sushi connoisseurs will appreciate Komazushi. Although master chef Takatomo Hachinohe died in 1998, Jun Sakamoto, the sushiman in charge, maintains the high standards set by his predecessor. The seats at the bar are reserved for customers known to order expensive options. *Rua São Carlos do Pinhal 241, Bela Vista, tel. 011/287–1820. No credit cards. Closed Mon. Metrô: Trianon.*

$–$$$$ NAKOMBI. A *Kombi* (Volkswagen van) in the middle of the dining room acts as a balcony where chefs prepare sushi. In this eclectic environment, tables are surrounded by a small artificial river crowded with fish. The menu includes a good variety of dishes. Try the salmon fillet with *shimeji* mushrooms. *Rua Pequetita 170, Vila Olímpia, tel. 011/3845–9911. AE, DC, MC, V.*

LEBANESE

$$–$$$$ ARÁBIA. For more than 10 years, Arábia has been serving traditional Lebanese cuisine in a beautiful, high-ceiling location. Simple dishes such as hummus and stuffed grape leaves are executed with aplomb. The lamb melts in your mouth with astonishing speed. The "executive" lunch includes one cold dish, one meat dish, a drink, and dessert—all at a (relatively) reasonable price. Don't miss the rose syrup for dessert; it comes over a pistachio delight that may leave you in tears. Rua Haddock Lobo 1397, Jardins, tel. 011/ 3061–2203, www.arabia.com.br. AE, DC, MC.

$ ALMANARA. Part of a chain of Lebanese semi–fast-food outlets,
★ Almanara is perfect for a quick lunch of hummus, tabbouleh, grilled chicken, and rice. There's also a full-blown restaurant on the premises that serves Lebanese specialties rodízio style (you get a taste of everything until you can ingest no more). Rua Oscar Freire 523, Jardins, tel. 011/3085–6916. AE, DC, MC, V.

PAN-ASIAN

$$–$$$ SUTRA. A coconut tree grows in the middle of this cozy bar–restaurant, a huge map of Thailand covers one wall, and sofas with pillows provide a comfy place to relax. The chic, creative mix of Asian cuisines includes Vietnamese, Thai, and Japanese. A recommended dish is kaeng kung (prawns with broccoli and other vegetables in a curry-and-coconut-milk sauce). To spice up your love life, you can choose from aphrodisiac drinks with names inspired by the Kama Sutra (tabletop cards even have illustrations). The "bamboo splitting," for example, is made of Absolut, tequila, Cointreau, lemon juice, and Coca Cola. Rua Salvador Cardoso 20, Itaim Bibi, tel. 011/3849–4758. DC, MC, V. Closed Sun.–Mon. No lunch.

$–$$$ ORIENTAL CAFÉ. High ceilings and tile floors convey a sense of space, while candles flickering on tables keep things intimate. With such sophisticated dishes as shark-fin soup, this is considered the best restaurant of its kind. You'll also find less exotic dishes such as marinated chicken thighs. Rua José Maria Lisboa 1000, Jardim Paulista, tel. 011/3060–9495. AE, DC, MC, V. Closed Mon. No lunch Tues.– Sat.

PIZZA

$–$$ GALPÃO. Owned by an architect, this pizzeria has such interesting
★ decor details as lights that shine from behind bottle bottoms
embedded in exposed brick walls. Fast service is also a hallmark.
The best menu choice is the arugula, sun-dried tomatoes, and
mozzarella pizza. *Rua Doutor Augusto de Miranda 1156, Pompéia,* tel.
011/3672–4767. DC, MC, V. Closed Mon.

$–$$ OFICINA DE PIZZAS. Both branches of this restaurant look like
something designed by the Spanish artist Gaudí, but the pizzas
couldn't be more Italian and straightforward. Try a pie with
mozzarella and toasted garlic. *Rua Purpurina 517, Vila Madalena,*
tel. 011/3816–3749. DC, MC, V. *Rua Inácio Pereira da Rocha 15, Vila
Madalena,* tel. 011/3813–8389. DC, MC, V.

$–$$ PIOLA. Part of a chain started in Italy, this restaurant serves good
pasta dishes as well as pizza. It's frequented by young people who
seem to match the trendy decoration perfectly. *Rua Oscar Freire 512,
Jardins,* tel. 011/3064–6570, *www.piola.com.br.* AE, DC, MC, V.

$–$$ PIZZARIA CAMELO. Though it's neither fancy nor beautiful, its
wide variety of thin-crust pies served has kept paulistanos
enthralled for ages. The *chopp* (draft beer) is great, too. Avoid
Sunday night, unless you want to wait an hour for a table. *Rua
Pamplona 1873, Cerqueira César,* tel. 011/3887–8764. DC, MC, V.

$–$$ SPERANZA. One of the most traditional pizzerias, this restaurant
is famous for its margherita pie. The crunchy *pão de linguiça*
(sausage bread) appetizers have a fine reputation as well. *Rua 13
de Maio 1004, Bela Vista,* tel. 011/288–8502. DC, MC, V.

$–$$ I VITELLONI. The pizza with arugula, mozzarella, sun-dried
tomatoes, and roasted garlic invented here has been copied by
pizzerias all over town. The place is small, but the service is great.
Rua Conde Sílvio Álvares Penteado 31, Pinheiros, tel. 011/3819–0735.
No credit cards.

SEAFOOD

$$–$$$$ AMADEUS. The quality and preparation of the fish is famous among the business lunch crowd. Appetizers such as fresh oysters and salmon and endive with mustard, and entrées like shrimp in a cognac sauce, make it a challenge to find better fruits of the sea elsewhere in town. *Rua Haddock Lobo 807, Jardins, tel. 011/3061–2859. AE, DC. No dinner weekends. Metrô: Consolação.*

$$–$$$$ TRUTA ROSA. Fresh trout, prepared in endless ways, makes this small restaurant with a huge fish-shape window a hit. You'll cross a metal bridge over a small lagoon to reach the dining room, where sashimi and quenelles reel in the customers. *Av. Vereador José Diniz 318, Santo Amaro, tel. 011/5523–7021. AE, DC, MC, V. Closed Mon. No dinner Sun.*

In This Chapter

Updated by Karla Brunet

shopping

PEOPLE COME FROM ALL OVER SOUTH AMERICA to shop in São Paulo, and shopping is considered an attraction in its own right by many paulistanos. In the Jardins neighborhood, stores that carry well-known brands from around the world alternate with the best Brazilian shops. Prices are high for most items, especially in Jardins and the major shopping centers.

Stores are open weekdays 9–6:30 and Saturday 9–1. A few are open on Sunday (for a list of these shops and their Sunday hours, call 011/210–4000 or 011/813–3311). Mall hours are generally weekdays 10–10 and Saturday 9 AM–10 PM; during gift-giving holiday seasons malls open on Sunday.

AREAS

In Centro, Rua do Arouche is noted for leather goods. In Itaim, the area around Rua João Cachoeira has evolved from a neighborhood of small clothing factories into a wholesale- and retail-clothing sales district. Several shops on Rua Tabapuã sell small antiques. Also, Rua Dr. Mário Ferraz is stuffed with elegant clothing, gift, and home-decoration stores. Jardins, centering on Rua Augusta (which crosses Avenida Paulista) and Rua Oscar Freire, is the chicest area. Double-parked Mercedes-Benzes and BMWs point the way to the city's fanciest stores, which sell leather items, jewelry, gifts, antiques, and art. You'll also find many restaurants and beauty salons. Shops that specialize in high-price European antiques are on or around Rua da

Consolação. A slew of lower-price antiques stores line Rua Cardeal Arcoverde in Pinheiros.

CENTERS AND MALLS

D&D DECORAÇÃO & DESIGN CENTER. This complex shares a building with the world trade center and the Gran Meliá hotel. It's loaded with fancy decoration stores, full-scale restaurants, and fast-food spots. *Av. das Nações Unidas 12555, Brooklin Novo, tel. 011/3043–9000.*

SHOPPING CENTER IBIRAPUERA. For a long time the largest shopping mall in Brazil, Ibirapuera features more than 500 stores in addition to three movie theaters. *Av. Ibirapuera 3103, Moema, tel. 011/5095–2300.*

SHOPPING CENTER IGUATEMI. The city's oldest and most sophisticated mall offers the latest in fashion and fast food. Four movie theaters often show American films in English with Portuguese subtitles. The Gero Café, built in the middle of the main hall, has a fine menu. *Av. Brigadeiro Faria Lima 2232, Jardim Paulista, tel. 011/3816–6116.*

SHOPPING CENTER MORUMBI. Set in the city's fastest-growing area, Morumbi is giving Iguatemi a run for its money. That said, it houses about the same boutiques, record stores, bookstores, and restaurants as Iguatemi, though it has more movie theaters (a total of six). *Av. Roque Petroni Jr. 1089, Morumbi, tel. 0800/17–7600.*

MARKETS

Almost every neighborhood has a weekly outdoor food market (days are listed in local newspapers), complete with loudmouthed hawkers, exotic scents, and piles of colorful produce.

On Sunday, there are **ANTIQUES FAIRS** near the Museu de Arte de São Paulo and (in the afternoon) at the Shopping Center Iguatemi's parking lot. Many stall owners have shops and hand out business cards so you can browse throughout the week at your leisure. An **ARTS AND CRAFTS FAIR**—selling jewelry, embroidery, leather goods, toys, clothing, paintings, and musical instruments—takes place Sunday morning in Centro's Praça da República. Many booths move over to the nearby Praça da Liberdade in the afternoon, joining vendors there selling Japanese-style ceramics, wooden sandals, cooking utensils, food, and bonsai trees. **FLEA MARKETS**—with second-hand furniture, clothes, and CDs—take place on Saturday at Praça Benedito Calixto in Pinheiros and on Sunday at the Praça Dom Orione in Bela Vista.

SPECIALTY SHOPS

Antiques

ANTIQUÁRIO PAULO VASCONCELOS. Folk art and 18th- and 19th-century Brazilian furniture are among the finds here. *Alameda Gabriel Monteiro da Silva 1881, Jardins, tel. 011/3062–2444.*

EDWIN LEONARD. This collective of three dealers sells Latin American and European antiques. *Rua Oscar Freire 146, Jardins, tel. 011/3088–1394.*

PATRIMÔNIO. Come for Brazilian antiques at reasonable prices. It also sells some Indian artifacts as well as modern furnishings crafted from iron. *Alameda Ministro Rocha Azevedo 1068, Jardins, tel. 011/3064–1750.*

RENATO MAGALHÃES GOUVÊA ESCRITÓRIO DE ARTE. This shop offers a potpourri of European and Brazilian antiques, modern furnishings, and art. *Av. Europa 68, Jardins, tel. 011/3081–2166.*

Art

ARTE APLICADA. For Brazilian paintings, sculptures, and prints, this is the place. *Rua Haddock Lobo 1406, Jardins, tel. 011/3062–5128.*

CAMARGO VILAÇA. The staff has an eye for the works of up-and-coming Brazilian artists. *Rua Fradique Coutinho 1500, Vila Madalena, tel. 011/3032–7066.*

ESPAÇO CULTURAL ENA BEÇAK. You can shop for Brazilian prints, sculptures, and paintings and then stop in the café. *Rua Oscar Freire 440, Jardins, tel. 011/3088–7322.*

GALERIA JACQUES ARDIES. If art naïf is your thing, this place is a must. *Rua do Livramento 221, Vila Mariana, tel. 011/3884–2916. Metrô: Paraíso.*

GALERIA RENOT. Here you'll find oil paintings by such Brazilian artists as Vicente Rego Monteiro, Di Cavalcanti, Cícero Dias, and Anita Malfatti. *Alameda Ministro Rocha Azevedo 1327, Jardins, tel. 011/3083–5933.*

GALERIA SÃO PAULO. This gallery is a leader in contemporary, mainstream art. *Rua Estados Unidos 1456, Jardins, tel. 011/3062–8855.*

MÔNICA FILGUEIRAS GALERIA. Many a trend has been set at this gallery. *Alameda Ministro Rocha Azevedo 927, Jardins, tel. 011/3082–5292.*

Clothing

ALEXANDRE HERCHOVITCH. Senhor Herchovitch is a famous Brazilian designer. His store has prêt-à-porter and tailor-made clothes. *Alameda Franca 631, Jardins, tel. 011/288–8005.*

ANACAPRI. This shop sells women's underwear, swimsuits, and clothes in large sizes. *Rua Juquis 276, Moema, tel. 011/5531–8913.*

CORI. Everyday outfits with classic lines are the specialty. *Rua Haddock Lobo 1584, Jardins, tel. 011/3081–5223.*

DASLU. You can mingle with elite ladies who enjoy personalized attention in this "closed" (no storefront) designer-label boutique. *Rua Domingos Leme 284, Vila Nova Conceição, tel. 011/3842–3785.*

ELITE. Owned by the modeling agency of the same name, this store is a favorite among girls from 13 years old and up for dresses and sportswear. *Rua Oscar Freire 735, Jardins, tel. 011/3082–9449.*

ELLUS. This is a good place to buy men's and women's jeans, sportswear, and street wear. *Shopping Eldorado, 3rd floor, Cerqueira César, tel. 011/3815–4554, www.ellus.com.br.*

FÓRUM. Although it has a lot of evening attire for young men and women, this shop also sells sportswear and shoes. *Rua Bela Cintra 2102, Jardins, tel. 011/3085–6269.*

LE LIS BLANC. This shop is Brazil's exclusive purveyor of the French brand Vertigo. Look for party dresses in velvet and sheer fabrics. *Rua Oscar Freire 809, Jardins, tel. 011/3083–2549.*

MARIA BONITA/MARIA BONITA EXTRA. If you have a little money in your pocket, shop at Maria Bonita, which has elegant women's clothes with terrific lines. At Maria Bonita Extra, the prices are a little lower. *Rua Oscar Freire 702, Jardins, tel. 011/3062–6433.*

PETISTIL. Younger family members aren't forgotten at this store, which sells clothes for infants and children up to 11 years old. *Rua Teodoro Sampaio 2271, Pinheiros, tel. 011/3816–2865.*

REINALDO LOURENÇO. The women's clothes here are high quality and sophisticated. *Rua Bela Cintra 2167, Jardins, tel. 011/3085–8150.*

RICHARD'S. This store carries one of Brazil's best lines of sportswear. Its collection includes outfits suitable for the beach or the mountains. *Rua Oscar Freire 1129, Jardins, tel. 011/3082–5399. Metrô: Consolação.*

UMA. Young women are intrigued by the unique designs of the swimsuits, dresses, shorts, shirts, and pants sold here. *Rua Girassol 273, Vila Madalena, tel. 011/3813–5559, www.uma.com.br.*

VILA ROMANA FACTORY STORE. You can't beat the prices for suits, jackets, jeans, and some women's wear (silk blouses, for example) at this store, a 40-minute drive from Centro. The in-town branch is more convenient, but its prices are higher. *Via Anhanguera, Km 17.5, tel. 011/3601–2211. Rua Oscar Freire 697, Jardins, tel. 011/3081–2919, www.vilaromana.com.br.*

VIVA VIDA. Long evening dresses—many done in shiny, sexy, exotic fabrics—steal the show. *Rua Oscar Freire 969, Jardins, tel. 011/3088–0421, www.vivavida.com.br.*

ZOOMP. This shop is famous for its jeans and high-quality street wear. Customers from 13 to 35 mix and match the clothes, creating some unusual combinations. *Rua Oscar Freire 995, Jardins, tel. 011/3064–1556, www.zoomp.com.br.*

Handicrafts

ALFÂNDEGA. The owners travel the world collecting things to sell in their shop. Just about every continent is represented, with such items as Indonesian dolls, painted Spanish bottles, Brazilian pottery, and candles. *Pátio Higienópolis, Av. Higienópolis 618, Loja 450, Higienópolis, tel. 011/3662–4651.*

ART ÍNDIA. This government-run shop sells Indian arts and crafts made by tribes throughout Brazil. *Rua Augusta 1371, Loja 119, Cerqueira César, tel. 011/283–2102. Metrô: Consolação.*

CASA DO AMAZONAS. As its name suggests, you'll find a wide selection of products from the Amazon in this store. *Galeria Metropôle, Av. São Luís 187, Loja 14, Centro, tel. 011/5051–3098. Metrô: São Luís.*

GALERIA DE ARTE BRASILEIRA. This shop specializes in Brazilian handicrafts. Look for objects made of pau-brasil wood, hammocks, jewelry, T-shirts, *marajoara* pottery (from the Amazon), and lace. *Alameda Lorena 2163, Jardins, tel. 011/3062–9452.*

Jewelry..

ANTÔNIO BERNARDO. One of Brazil's top designers owns this store; his work includes both modern and classic pieces that use only precious stones. *Rua Bela Cintra 2063, Jardins, tel. 011/3083–5622.*

ATELIER CECÍLIA RODRIGUES. This designer crafts unique pieces of gold and precious stones. *Rua Horácio Lafer 767, Itaim Bibi, tel. 011/3849–9393.*

CASTRO BERNARDES. In addition to selling jewelry and precious stones, this store restores old pieces. *Rua Jerônimo da Veiga 164, 19th floor, Itaim Bibi, tel. 011/3167–1001.*

In This Chapter

Updated by Karla Brunet

outdoor activities and sports

SÃO PAULO MAY NOT HAVE THE SAME REPUTATION for outdoor frollicking as Rio, but there are still plenty of opportunities for sport, from bicycling to scuba diving. If golf or tennis isn't your thing, you can always play spectator at a *futebol* (soccer) match, though those can be as heart-stopping as scaling one of the city's many indoor rock-climbing walls.

PARTICIPANT SPORTS

Bicycling

NIGHT BIKER'S CLUB (Rua Pacheco de Miranda 141, Jardim Paulista, tel. 011/3887–4773) offers bike tours of the city at night. **PARQUE IBIRAPUERA** has places that rent bicycles for about R$8 an hour and a special bike path. There are also bike lanes on Avenida Sumaré and Avenida Pedroso de Morais. **SAMPA BIKERS** (Rua São Sebastião 454, Chácara Santo Antônio, tel. 011/9990–0083 or 011/5183–9477) offers tours in the city and excursions outside town. A day tour costs about R$60, including transport and lunch.

Climbing

Inspired, perhaps, by the skyscrapers on Avenida Paulista, climbers have recently crowded the gyms and rock-climbing schools that have sprung up around town. Most places offer training and rent equipment. At **CASA DE PEDRA** (Rua da Paz

1823, Chácara Santo Antônio, tel. 011/5181–7873) the daily fee for using the rock-climbing facilities is R$20, and an hour of instruction is R$30. **JUMP** (Av. Pompéia 568, Pompéia, tel. 011/3675–2300) offers a three-day climbing course on its open walls. **90 GRAUS** (Rua João Pedro Cardoso 107, Aeroporto, tel. 011/5034–8775) opened in 1993 and offers climbing courses and individual training.

Golf

The greens fee at the 18-hole **CLUBE DE CAMPO** (Praça Rockford 28, Vila Represa, tel. 011/5929–3111) is R$50. It's open Monday–Tuesday and Thursday–Friday 7–7. **GOLF SCHOOL** (Av. Guido Caloi 2160, Santo Amaro, tel. 011/5515–3372) is a driving range that offers 30-minute classes for R$20; R$10 gets you 100 balls.

Scuba Diving

Most dive schools take you to Ilhabela and other places outside town on weekends and offer NAUI and PADI certification courses. **CLAUMAR** (Av. Brigadeiro Faria Lima 4440, Itaim Bibi, tel. 011/3846–3034) has a 15-m (49-ft) diving tower used during classes in São Paulo. **DEEP SEA** (Rua Manoel da Nóbrega 781, Paraíso, tel. 011/3889–7721) has small group dive trips to Lage de Santos in a fast boat. **DIVING COLLEGE** (Rua Doutor Mello Alves 700, Cerqueira César, tel. 011/3061–1453) is one of the oldest diving schools in Brazil and offers all the PADI courses.

Tennis

Court fees at **PLAY TÊNIS** (Leopoldo Couto de Magalhães Jr. 1097, Itaim Bibi, tel. 011/3845–7446) are R$35 an hour, but they don't rent rackets. **TÊNIS COACH** (Rua Dr. Francisco Tomás de Carvalho 940, Morumbi) rents courts and and has classes for people of all ages.

SPECTATOR SPORTS

Auto Racing

São Paulo hosts a Formula I race every March, bringing this city of 4.5 million cars to heights of spontaneous combustion, especially when a Brazilian driver wins. The race is held at **AUTÓDROMO DE INTERLAGOS** (Av. Senador Teotônio Vilela 315, Interlagos, tel. 011/5521–9911), which also hosts other kinds of races on weekends. For ticket information on the Formula I race contact the **CONFEDERAÇÃO BRASILEIRA DE AUTOMOBILISMO** (Rua da Glória 290, 8th floor, Rio de Janeiro, RJ 20241-180, tel. 021/2221–4895).

Futebol

Futebol (soccer) has always been a Brazilian passion. The nation's love affair with the sport became even stronger after Brazil won the 1994 World Cup and has reached the finals in subsequent years. São Paulo has several well-funded teams with some of the country's best players. The five main teams—São Paulo, Palmeiras, Portuguesa, Corinthians, and Juventus—even attract fans from other states. The two biggest stadiums are Morumbi and the municipally run Pacaembu. Note that covered seats offer the best protection, not only from the elements but also from rowdy spectators.

MORUMBI (Praça Roberto Gomes Pedrosa, Morumbi, tel. 011/3749–8000), the home stadium of São Paulo Futebol Clube, has a capacity of 85,000. The first games of the 1950 World Cup were played at the **PACAEMBU** (Praça Charles Miller, Pacaembu, tel. 011/3661–9111) stadium.

Horse Racing

Thoroughbreds race at the **SÃO PAULO JOCKEY CLUB** (Rua Lineu de Paula Machado 1263, Cidade Jardim, tel. 011/3816–4011), which is open Monday and Wednesday–Thursday 7:30 PM–11:30 PM and weekends 2–9. Card-carrying Jockey Club members get the best seats and have access to the elegant restaurant.

In This Chapter

Updated by Karla Brunet

nightlife and the arts

SÃO PAULO MAY BE BEST KNOWN FOR BUSINESS, but when the day is done, paulistanos like to party just as hard as their counterparts in Rio. The city's nightlife is as diverse as it's population: you'll find swanky lounges, discos, karaoke bars, and clubs offering blues, jazz, rock, and every type of Brazilian music. Of course, a city as cosmopolitan as São Paulo has no shortage of high profile theatrical and cultural events, including an international film festival.

NIGHTLIFE

São Paulo is a city beset by trends, so clubs and bars come and go at a dizzying pace. Though these were all thriving spots at press time, it's best to check with hotel concierges and paulistanos you meet to confirm that a place is still open before heading out on the town.

Bars

From the sophisticated to the casual, there is a bar for every taste. The most expensive places are in the Itaim neighborhood. Vila Madalena is full of trendy places.

BALCÃO. The word for "balcony" in Portuguese is *balcão*, and true to its name, this place has a sprawling one. If you'd like a little food to accompany your drinks and conversation, try the sun-dried tomato and mozzarella sandwich. *Rua Doutor Melo Alves 150, Jardim Paulista, tel. 011/3088–4630. Metrô: Consolação.*

BAR BRAHMA. First opened in 1949, this used to be the meeting place of artists, intellectuals and politicians. It was closed down in 1997, but reopened in 2001 and is again a popular place to meet. *Av. São João 677, Centro, tel. 011/3333–0855.*

BARNALDO LUCRÉCIA. Live *música popular brasileira* (MPB; popular Brazilian music) is often a draw. The crowd is intense though jovial. *Rua Abílio Soares 207, Paraíso, tel. 011/3885–3425. Metrô: Paraíso.*

ELIAS. This place is a hangout for fans of the Palmeiras soccer team, whose stadium is just a few blocks away. If you want something to eat, the carpaccio is undoubtedly the best choice on the menu. *Rua Cayowaá 70, Perdizes, tel. 011/3864–4722.*

EMPANADAS. Most patrons stop for a beer en route to another Vila Madalena bar. It's a good place to "warm up" for an evening out with a quick drink and a bite to eat. The empanadas are particularly appealing. *Rua Wisard 489, Vila Madalena, tel. 011/3032–2116.*

FRANGÓ. Because it's set in the Freguesia do Ó neighborhood, a stop makes you feel as if you've been transported to a small town. In addition to a pleasant location, Frangó also offers 90 varieties of beer, including the Brazilian export beer Xingu. Its rich, molasseslike flavor nicely complements the bar's unforgettable *bolinhos de frango com queijo* (chicken balls with cheese). *Largo da Matriz de Nossa Senhora do Ó 168, Freguesia do Ó, tel. 011/3932–4818 or 011/3931–4281.*

GRAZIE A DIO. The patrons may be different ages, but they're usually fashionable and always like good music. The best time to go is at happy hour for daily live performances. On Saturday it's jazz, and on Friday, bossa nova. The natural decorations, including trees and constellations, complement the Mediterranean food served in the back. *Rua Girassol 67, Vila Madalena, tel. 011/3031–6568.*

ORIGINAL. This place was one of the first of many bars modeled on 1940s-era Rio clubs. It has good draft beer and snacks. *Rua Graúna 137, Moema, tel.* 011/530–9486.

PIRAJÁ. The pictures of Rio de Janeiro on the walls will make you think fondly of Ipanema. The action starts at happy hour after 6 PM. *Av. Brigadeiro Faria Lima 64, Pinheiros, tel.* 011/3815–6881.

Brazilian Clubs

MPB clubs book quiet, largely acoustic instrumental and vocal music in the style of Milton Nascimento, Chico Buarque, and Gilberto Gil. The emphasis tends to be on samba and bossa nova.

PIRATININGA. The tiny round tables at this small bar-restaurant are perfect for a quiet rendezvous. The live MPB and jazz music add to the romance. *Rua Wizard 149, Vila Madalena, tel.* 011/3032–9775.

SEM EIRA NEM BEIRA. The decor was inspired by Brazilian bars circa 1940. Previously called Vou Vivendo, the club is famous for its live MPB performances on Friday and Saturday. *Rua Fiandeiras 966, Itaim Bibi, tel.* 011/3845–3444.

Cybercafés

ESPAÇO IDEAL. You can keep up with your stocks on the six computers, which have Internet access and are connected to a printer. It costs R$4 for a half hour and R$7 for an hour. There's also a good selection of healthy sandwiches, juices, and coffee to satisfy your body as well as your mind. *Rua Artur de Azevedo 1339, Pinheiros, tel.* 011/3081–9670.

FRANS CAFÉ AT FNAC. Inside a well-known French store you'll find six computers connected Monday–Sunday 10–10. Access costs about R$4 for a half hour and R$7 per hour. *Av. Pedroso de Morais 858, Pinheiros, tel.* 011/3814–2404.

B.A.S.E./DIESEL. The space-age decor puts you in the mood for a little cyber-exploration. For R$6 per half hour, you can log onto one of eight computers Tuesday–Friday after 10 PM and Saturday after 11 PM, when this dance club is in full swing. *Av. Brigadeiro Luiz Antônio 1137, Bela Vista, tel. 011/3106–3244.*

COFFEE & BOOK AT SARAIVA MEGASTORE. This store sells CDs and books and has a café as well as five computers. You can log on Monday–Saturday 10–10 and Sunday 2–8; the cost is R$5 for the first half hour and R$4 for each additional 30 minutes. *Shopping Eldorado, Av. Rebouças 3970, Pinheiros, tel. 011/3819–1770.*

Dance Clubs

People tend to go dancing very late. Still, you should arrive early to avoid the lines. Don't worry if the dance floor appears empty at 11 PM; things will start to sizzle an hour or so later.

AVENIDA CLUB. Some nights are dedicated to Caribbean rhythms, others to MPB. Regardless, the large wooden dance floor—one of the finest in town—attracts a crowd of thirtysomethings. *Av. Pedroso de Morais 1036, Pinheiros, tel. 011/3814–7383.*

B.A.S.E./DIESEL. In the '60s this was a bathhouse, but now it hosts hot dance parties from 9 PM until the wee hours. Three bars and an enormous dance floor reverberate to a mix of everything from Jimi Hendrix to cutting-edge dance hits. *Av. Brigadeiro Luíz Antônio 1137, Bela Vista, tel. 011/3106–3244.*

BLEN BLEN BRASIL. You can dance to live music—from reggae to salsa to Brazilian rock. *Rua Inácio Pereira da Rocha 520, Pinheiros, tel. 011/3812–2890.*

BRANCALEONE. Even if you've always been told that you move to the beat of a different drum, you'll find a suitable rhythm here. Each night brings a new beat, including disco, rock, funk, soul, Brazilian pop, and forró. You can take a break on the patio; refreshments include food as well as drink. *Rua Luis Murat 298, Jardim América, tel. 011/3819–8873.*

CANTO DA EMA. Considered the best place to dance forró in town, here you'll find people of different ages and styles coming together on the dance floor. *Xiboquinha* is the official forró drink, made with *cachaça* (a Brazilian sugarcane-based alcohol), lemon, honey, cinnamon, and ginger. *Av. Brigadeiro Faria Lima 364, Pinheiros, tel. 011/3813–4708.*

CARIOCA CLUB. *Carioca* is the name for a person from Rio de Janeiro, and this place has the decor of old-style Rio clubs. Its large dance floor attracts an eclectic mix of college students, couples, and professional dancers who move to samba, *axé* (a type of music from Bahia), and pagode. *Rua Cardeal Arcoverde 2899, Pinheiros, tel. 011/3812–3782.*

DOLORES BAR. DJs spin funk, soul, and hip-hop tunes for a crowd in its twenties and thirties. Wednesday and Friday nights are the most popular, and people really do fill up the floor only after the witching hour. *Rua Fradique Coutinho 1007, Vila Madalena, tel. 011/3031–3604.*

KVA. Live or recorded forró is played every night. There are three stages, two dance floors, and one coffee shop. *Rua Cardeal Arcoverde 2958, Pinheiros, tel. 011/3819–2153.*

A LANTERNA. Because this venue is a mixture of restaurant, bar, and nightclub, you can go early for dinner and stay late for dancing. Actors, dancers, and musicians give performances that add to the entertainment. The walls are decorated with local artists' works. *Rua Fidalga 531, Vila Madalena, tel. 011/3816–0904.*

LOV.E CLUB & LOUNGE. The interior design makes you feel like you're in a set from an *Austin Powers* movie. Before 2 AM the music isn't too loud, and you can sit and talk on the '50s-style sofas. Then the techno effects keep people on the small dance floor until sunrise. *Rua Pequetita 189, Vila Olímpia, tel. 011/3044–1613.*

NIAS. This is one of the few places left where you can still dance to true rock and roll. DJs play tunes from the '80s and '90s and also current international pop-rock tunes. *Rua dos Pinheiros 688, Pinheiros, tel. 011/3062–3877.*

THE POOL. Ever wish you could fully cool off during a hot night of dancing? Well, this place has a 8-m-long (26-ft-long) pool where you can do just that. The club will provide you with a swimsuit, but you can't wear it back on the dance floor. DJs play house music. *Rua Teodoro Sampaio 1109, Pinheiros, tel. 011/3068–8307.*

Gay and Lesbian Clubs

A LÔCA. You'll find a large dance floor, a video room, and two bars here. A mixed gay and lesbian crowd often dances until dawn and then has breakfast in the club. *Rua Frei Caneca 916, Cerqueira César, tel. 011/3120–2055. Metrô: Consolação.*

MASSIVO. This fabulous underground disco and club welcomes gay, lesbian, and straight patrons. *Rua Alameda Itu 1548, Jardins, tel. 011/3083–7505. Metrô: Consolação.*

MUZIK. This place is frequented mostly by men between the ages of 18 and 35, and there's room for 1,200 of them. Bodybuilders in swim trunks dance on stages while DJ Mauro Borges and others play '70s and house music until the last patron leaves. *Rua da Consolação 3032, Jardim Paulista, tel. 011/3081–5496.*

STEREO. The fashionable and exotic crowd is primarily gay, but straight patrons meet to dance as well. Decorations have a retro-futuristic look. Be prepared for a mob on Wednesday, which is '80s night. *Alameda Olga 168, Barra Funda, tel. 011/3664–7925. Metrô: Barra Funda.*

Jazz Clubs

ALL OF JAZZ. People come to this small place to actually listen to very good jazz and bossa nova. Local musicians jam here weekly. Call ahead to book a table on weekends. *Rua João Cachoeira 1366, Vila Olímpia, tel. 011/3849–1345.*

BOURBON STREET. With a name right out of New Orleans, one of the world's coolest jazz towns, it's no wonder this is where the best jazz and blues bands play. *Rua Dos Chanés 127, Moema, tel. 011/5561–1643.*

CAFÉ PIU PIU. Although this establishment is best known for jazz, it also hosts groups that play rock, bossa nova, and even tango. Decorations include statues, an antique balcony, and marble tables. *Rua 13 de Maio 134, Bixiga, tel. 011/258–8066.*

MR. BLUES JAZZ BAR. At this traditional jazz, blues, and soul venue, the audience drinks beer and whiskey and eats french fries with Parmesan cheese. *Av. São Gabriel 558, Jardim Paulista, tel. 011/3884–9356.*

SANJA JAZZ BAR. A few tables (arrive early to get a seat) in an old town house are the setting for live jazz, rock, and blues performances. *Rua Frei Caneca 304, Consolação, tel. 011/255–2942.*

THE ARTS

The world's top orchestras, opera and dance companies, and other troupes always include São Paulo in their South American tours. Listings of events appear in the "Veja São Paulo" insert of the newsweekly *Veja.* The arts sections of the dailies *Folha de São Paulo* and *O Estado de São Paulo* also have listings and reviews. In addition, *Folha* publishes a weekly guide on Friday called "Guia da Folha."

Tickets for many events are available at booths throughout the city as well as at theater box offices Many of these venues offer ticket delivery for a surcharge. **FUN BY PHONE** (tel. 011/3097–8687) sells ticket to music concerts, theater, and theme parks. **LUCAS SHOWS** (tel. 011/3858–5783) delivers tickets to your hotel door for a fee. At **SHOW TICKET AT SHOPPING CENTER IGUATEMI** (Av. Brigadeiro Faria Lima 1191, 3rd floor, tel. 011/3814–9807) you can buy tickets to the main concerts and performances in town Monday–Saturday 10–10 and Sunday 2–8.

Classical Music, Dance, and Theater

The city is home to both a state and a municipal orchestra, though both suffer from a chronic lack of funds. The theater district, in the bohemian Bela Vista neighborhood, has dozens of theaters dedicated mostly to plays in Portuguese. The contemporary music ensemble **GRUPO NOVO HORIZONTE** (tel. 011/256–9766), a group of eight professional musicians, gives performances in town but does not have a permanent home.

PERFORMANCE VENUES

SALA SÃO LUIZ. This venue hosts chamber music performances. *Av. Juscelino Kubitschek 1830, Itaim Bibi, tel. 011/3847–4111.*

TEATRO ALFA. Opera, ballet, music, and symphony performances are held here. It's one of the newest theaters in the country, with all the latest sound and lighting technology—and the biggest foreign stars grace the stage. Tickets can be bought by phone and picked up a half hour before the performance. *Rua Bento Branco de Andrade Filho 722, Santo Amaro, tel. 011/5693–4000 or 0800/55–8191, www.teatroalfa.com.br.*

TEATRO CULTURA ARTÍSTICA. Its fine acoustics make this theater perfect for classical music performances. It also hosts dance recitals and plays. *Rua Nestor Pestana 196, Cerqueira César, tel. 011/258–3616, www.culturaartistica.com.br.*

TEATRO FACULDADE ARMANDO ÁLVARES PENTEADO (FAAP). The FAAP Theater presents concerts and Brazilian plays. *Rua Alagoas 903, Pacaembú, tel. 011/3662–1992.*

TEATRO JOÃO CAETANO. This theater hosts state-sponsored festivals as well as Brazilian plays. *Rua Borges Lagoa 650, Vila Mariana, tel. 011/5573–3774. Metrô: Santa Cruz.*

TEATRO MUNICIPAL. Most serious music, ballet, and opera is performed in the intimate gilt and moss-green-velvet surroundings of this classic theater. There are lyrical performances on Monday evenings at 8:30 and concerts on

Wednesday afternoons at 12:30. A local cultural organization, the Mozarteum Brasileira Associação Cultural, holds classical music concerts, which include performances by visiting artists, April–October. *Praça Ramos de Azevedo, Centro, tel. 011/ 222–8698. Metrô: Anhangabaú.*

TUCA. The Catholic University theater puts on alternative concerts as well as plays. *Rua Monte Alegre 1024, Sumaré, tel. 011/ 3670–8453.*

VIA FUNCHAL. Capable of seating more than 3,000 people, this is the site of many large international shows. *Rua Funchal 65, Vila Olímpia, tel. 011/3846–2300 or 011/3842–6855, www.viafunchal. com.br.*

Escola de Samba

From December through February, many *escolas de samba* (samba "schools"—groups that perform during Carnaval) open their rehearsals to the public. Drummers get in sync with the singers, and everyone learns the lyrics to each year's songs. **ROSAS DE OURO** (Av. Cel. Euclides Machado 1066, Freguesia do Ó, tel. 011/3966–0608 or 011/3857–4555) has one of the most popular escola de samba rehearsals.

Film

Only foreign children's movies are dubbed; the rest have subtitles with the original dialogue intact. Arrive at blockbuster releases at least 40 minutes early, particularly on Sunday night. The region near Avenida Paulista, Avenida Consolação, and Rua Augusta has more than 10 movie theaters as well as many cafés and bars where you can hang out before or after the show. Movie theaters in shopping centers are also good options. Call ahead for confirmation because theaters often change their programming without notice.

The **BELAS ARTES** complex (Rua da Consolação 2423, Consolação, tel. 011/258–4092 or 011/259–6341) offers Hollywood films. **CENTRO CULTURAL SÃO PAULO** (Rua Vergueiro 1000, Paraíso, tel. 011/3277–3611, ext. 279) usually features a series of theme films for free or nearly free. It also presents plays, concerts, and art exhibits. **CINEARTE** (Av. Paulista 2073, Jardim Paulista, tel. 011/285–3696) hosts most of the premieres in town. Brazilian, European, and other non-American films are shown at the **ESPAÇO UNIBANCO** (Rua Augusta 1470/1475, Consolação, tel. 011/288–6780).

Free Shows

Most free concerts—with performances by either Brazilian or international artists—are presented on Sunday in Parque Ibirapuera. City-sponsored events are held in Centro's Vale do Anhangabaú area. State-sponsored concerts take place at the Memorial da América Latina, northwest of Centro. **SERVIÇO SOCIAL DO COMÉRCIO** (SESC, Commerce Social Service; tel. 011/3179–3400) is very active in cultural programming, and many of its events are free. The organization has units in several neighborhoods.

Not a Night Owl?

You can learn a lot about a place if you take its pulse after dark. So even if you're the original early-to-bed type, there's every reason to vary your routine when you're away from home.

EXPERIENCE THE FAMILIAR IN A NEW PLACE Whether your thing is going to the movies or going to concerts, it's always different away from home. In clubs, new faces and new sounds add up to a different scene. Or you may catch movies you'd never see at home.

TRY SOMETHING NEW Do something you've never done before. It's another way to dip into the local scene. A simple suggestion: Go out later than usual—go dancing late and finish up with breakfast at dawn.

DO SOMETHING OFFBEAT Look into lectures and readings as well as author appearances in book stores. You may even meet your favorite novelist.

EXPLORE A DAYTIME NEIGHBORHOOD AT NIGHT Take a nighttime walk through an explorable area you've already seen by day. You'll get a whole different view of it.

ASK AROUND If you strike up a conversation with like-minded people during the course of your day, ask them about their favorite spots. Your hotel concierge is another resource.

DON'T WING IT As soon as you've nailed down your travel dates, look into local publications or surf the Net to see what's on the calendar while you're in town. Look for hot regional acts, dance and theater, big-name performing artists, expositions, and sporting events. Then call or click to order tickets.

CHECK OUT THE NEIGHBORHOOD Whenever you don't know the neighborhood you'll be visiting, review safety issues with people in your hotel. What's the transportation situation? Can you walk there, or do you need a cab? Is there anything else you need to know?

CASH OR CREDIT? Know before you go. It's always fun to be surprised—but not when you can't cover your check.

In This Chapter

Updated by Karla Brunet

where to stay

SÃO PAULO'S HOTELS ARE ALMOST EXCLUSIVELY geared to business travelers, both homegrown and foreign. For this reason, most hotels are near Avenida Paulista, with a few in the Marginal Pinheiros and charming Jardins neighborhoods.

For information about youth hostels, contact the **ASSOCIAÇÃO PAULISTA DE ALBERGUES DA JUVENTUDE** (Rua 7 de Abril 386, República, 01320-040, tel. 011/258–0388). The association sells a book ($2.50) that lists hostels throughout Brazil.

PRICES

Many hotels offer discounts of 20%–40% for cash payment or weekend stays. Few include breakfast in the room rate. São Paulo hosts many international conventions, so it's wise to make reservations well ahead of your arrival.

CATEGORY	COST*
$$$$	over R$400
$$$	R$300–R$400
$$	R$200–R$300
$	R$100–R$200
¢	under R$100

for a double room in high season, excluding taxes

$$$$ ★ **GRAN MELIÁ SÃO PAULO.** The Meliá is in the same building as São Paulo's world trade center and the D&D Decoração & Design Center. Off the large marble lobby is a bar whose comfortable leather chairs are perfect for unwinding after a day of meetings or shopping. Guest rooms have king-size beds, two phone lines, living rooms with sofas, and small tables that are the perfect places to set up your laptop. The apartment floors have such special amenities as pass-key access and bathroom faucets that can be programmed to maintain whatever water temperature you prefer. *Av. das Nações Unidas 12559, Brooklin 04578-905, tel. 011/3043–8000 or 0800/15–5555, fax 011/3043–8001, www.solmelia.es. 300 suites. Restaurant, bar, in-room data ports, in-room safes, room service, indoor pool, hair salon, massage, sauna, tennis court, exercise room, paddle tennis, business services, meeting room. AE, DC, MC, V.*

$$$$ L'HOTEL. Close to the major business hubs, this European-style hotel has rooms and suites decorated in somewhat sterile floral patterns. The place was modeled after the famous L'Hotel in Paris, and the small number of rooms allows it to focus on providing superior service. Though at its inception L'Hotel wanted to retain an air of exclusivity, reports have been mixed as to its success. *Alameda Campinas 266, Jardins 01404-000, tel./fax 011/283–0500, www.lhotel.com.br. 82 rooms, 5 suites. 2 restaurants, pub, room service, pool, sauna, health club, business services, meeting room. AE, DC, MC, V. Metrô: Trianon.*

$$$$ HOTEL SOFITEL SÃO PAULO. Near the Congonhas Airport and Ibirapuera Park, this modern, luxury hotel is noted for its French style. The restaurant even serves French cuisine. *Rua Sena Madureira 1355, Bloco 1, Ibirapuera 04021-051, tel. 011/5574–1100 or 0800/11–1790, fax 011/5575–4544, www.accorbrasil.com.br. 219 rooms. Restaurant, bar, room service, pool, sauna, tennis court, exercise room, laundry, business services, meeting rooms. AE, DC, MC, V.*

$$$$ INTER-CONTINENTAL SÃO PAULO. This exquisite hotel is by far
★ the most attractive of the city's top-tier establishments. Service is attentive, and both the private and public areas are well appointed. Creams, pastels, and marble come together with seamless sophistication and elegance. *Av. Santos 1123, Jardins 01419-001, tel. 011/3179–2600, fax 011/3179–2666, www.interconti.com. 160 rooms, 33 suites. Restaurant, bar, room service, pool, massage,*

sauna, health club, business services, helipad. AE, DC, MC, V. Metrô: Trianon.

$$$$ RENAISSANCE SÃO PAULO. A stay at this Jardins hotel, a block from Avenida Paulista, puts you close to both shops and businesses. From the street, it has the appeal of a roll of tinfoil, but its interior is graceful and elegant. There are six Renaissance Club floors with 57 suites that include a buffet breakfast, evening hors d'oeuvres, butler service, express check-in and check-out, and fax machines. If you want to arrive in style, the hotel's helipad is key. *Alameda Santos 2247, Jardins 01419-002, tel. 011/3069–2233; 800/468–3571 in the U.S., fax 011/3064–3344, www.renaissancehotels.com. 452 rooms, 100 suites. 3 restaurants, 3 bars, room service, pool, massage, health club, squash, shops, business services, travel services, helipad, parking (fee). AE, DC, MC, V. Metrô: Consolação.*

$$$$ SHERATON MOFARREJ HOTEL & TOWERS. Just behind Avenida
★ Paulista and next to Parque Trianon, the Mofarrej is part of Sheraton's A-class Luxury Collection hotels. Rooms are done in light hues, and the four floors that have butler service offer other amenities that will make you feel all the more pampered. Rooms on the west side overlook the park. *Alameda Santos 1437, Jardins 01419-905, tel. 011/253–5544 or 0800/11–6000, fax 011/283–0160, www.sheraton-sp.com. 2 restaurants, 2 bars, room service, indoor pool, massage, sauna, exercise room, business services, convention center. AE, DC, MC, V. Metrô: Trianon.*

$$$$ TRANSAMÉRICA. Directly across the Rio Pinheiros from the Centro Empresarial office complex, the home of many U.S. companies, this hotel is a comfortable and convenient choice for those working outside Centro. The skylighted lobby has granite, marble, Persian carpets, palm trees, leather sofas, and oversize modern paintings; the spacious rooms have no special charm, but their pastel colors, wood furnishings, and beige carpeting create a relaxing atmosphere. *Av. das Nações Unidas 18591, Santo Amaro 04795-901, tel. 011/5693–4511 or 0800/12–6060, fax 011/5693–4990, www.transamerica.com.br. 396 rooms, 66 suites. Restaurant, bar,*

são paulo lodging

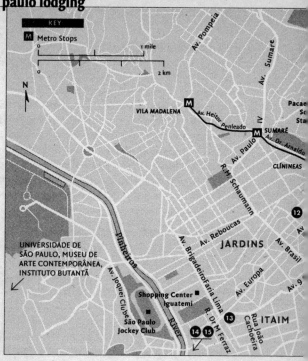

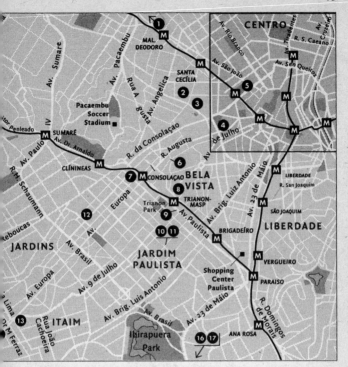

room service, pool, sauna, 9-hole golf course, 2 tennis courts, exercise room, jogging, business services. AE, DC, MC, V.

$$–$$$ MAKSOUD PLAZA. Ronald Reagan *almost* stayed here on a 1982 presidential visit, but the Secret Service thought the soaring atrium lobby—with its panoramic elevators, fountains, greenery, and shops—posed a security risk. The staff provides professional service, the hotel's restaurants aren't bad, and the in-house theater and the Maksoud 150 nightclub offer entertainment. *Alameda Campinas 1250, Jardins 01404-900, tel. 011/3145–8000, fax 011/3145–8001, www.maksoud.com.br. 416 rooms, 99 suites. 6 restaurants, 3 bars, room service, indoor pool, health club, nightclub, theater, business.*

$$ ELDORADO HIGIENÓPOLIS. Set in one of the city's oldest and
★ most attractive residential neighborhoods, only a five-minute taxi ride from Centro, this hotel has a large pool and a lobby dressed in travertine marble with a pink-granite floor. The on-site café is lovely, and the rooms are all pleasant; the noise level is lowest in those at the front above the fifth floor or those in back. *Rua Marquês de Itu 836, Higienópolis 01223-000, tel. 011/3361–6888, fax 011/222–7194, www.hoteiseldorado.com.br. 152 rooms. Restaurant, bar, room service, pool. AE, DC, MC, V.*

$$ GRANDE HOTEL CA' D'ORO. Owned and run by a northern Italian family for more than 40 years, this old world–style hotel near Centro has bar-side fireplaces, lots of wood and Persian carpeting, a great variety of room decor (all along classic European lines), ultrapersonalized service, and the beloved Ca' D'Oro restaurant. All these amenities attract many repeat customers, including quite a few Brazilian bigwigs. *Rua Augusta 129, Cerqueira César 01303-001, tel. 011/236–4300, fax 011/236–4311, www.cadoro.com.br. 240 rooms, 50 suites. Restaurant, 2 bars, room service, indoor pool, sauna, exercise room. AE, DC, MC, V. Metrô: Consolação.*

$–$$ BOURBON. Both guests and furnishings are well cared for in this small hotel near the Largo do Arouche, a charming downtown district. A brass-accented basement bar features live piano music.

The lobby has upholstered print sofas, an abstract handcrafted black-and-white wall hanging, and granite flooring. Rooms are done in beige and blue and have marvelously large, sunlit bathrooms. *Av. Vieira de Carvalho 99, Centro 01210-010, tel. 011/3337–2000, fax 011/220–8187. 123 rooms. Restaurant, bar, sauna. AE, DC, MC, V. Metrô: República.*

$ **CARILLON PLAZA.** Walk out of the heated hustle and bustle of the Jardins neighborhood and into this hotel's cool lobby full of mirrors and marble. You can retreat still farther by heading to the rooftop pool for an afternoon of sunbathing or by sinking into a leather chair for a meal in the restaurant. The multilingual staff is very helpful. *Rua Bela Cintra 652, Jardins 01415-000, tel. 011/257–9233, fax 011/255–3346, www.redepandehoteis.com.br/carillon/carillon.htm. 39 rooms, 10 suites. Restaurant, bar, in-room safes, room service, pool. AE, DC, MC, V. Metrô: Consolação.*

$ **NOVOTEL SÃO PAULO IBIRAPUERA.** Well located near Ibirapuera Park, with easy access to the city's main streets, Novotel São Paulo Ibirapuera offers solid service. In need of redecoration, it's still a decent choice, just not as great as it once was. *Rua Sena Madureira 1355, Ibirapuera 04021-051, tel. 011/5574–9099, fax 011/5572–3499. 80 rooms. Restaurant, bar, room service, pool, sauna, tennis court, exercise room, laundry, business services, meeting rooms. AE, DC, MC, V.*

$ **PARTHENON GOLDEN TOWER.** A full-service establishment with apartmentlike amenities, this hotel is popular with business travelers and families alike. The rooms are nicely decorated, and each has a private balcony. *Av. Cidade Jardim 411, Pinheiros 01453-000, tel. 011/3081–6333, fax 011/3088–3531, www.accorbrasil.com.br. 73 suites. Restaurant, bar, room service, pool, sauna, meeting room, exercise room, laundry. AE, DC, MC, V.*

¢–$ **LA GUARDIA.** If you don't need to be surrounded by luxury, consider this simple, affordable (compared with many establishments) hotel. Rooms are small but comfortable and have thick carpets and marble-top tables. The environment is friendly, and the service is good. *Rua Peixoto Gomide 154, Cerqueira César 01409-000, tel. 011/255-0600, fax 011/258-7398. 28 rooms, 14 suites. Restaurant, free parking. AE, DC, MC, V. Metrô: Consolação.*

¢–$ **VILLE HOTEL.** In the lively Higienópolis neighborhood of apartment buildings, bars, and bookstores abutting Mackenzie University, this hotel costs about R$90 a night. The small lobby features a black-and-pink-granite floor, recessed lighting, and leather sofas; rooms are done in pastels with brown carpeting. *Rua Dona Veridiana 643, Higienópolis 01238-010, tel. 011/257-5288, tel./fax 011/239-1871. 54 rooms. Restaurant, meeting room. AE, DC, MC, V.*

¢ **IBIS SÃO PAULO EXPO.** This large hotel has clean, budget rooms. The decoration is contemporary and functional. *Rua Eduardo Viana 163, Barra Funda 01133-040, tel. 011/3824-7373, fax 011/3824-7374. 280 rooms. Restaurant, room service, laundry, meeting rooms. AE, DC, MC, V.*

Hotel How-Tos

Where you stay does make a difference. Do you prefer a modern high-rise or an intimate B&B? A center-city location or the quiet suburbs? What facilities do you want? Sort through your priorities, then price it all out.

HOW TO GET A DEAL After you've chosen a likely candidate or two, phone them directly and price a room for your travel dates. Then call the hotel's toll-free number and ask the same questions. Also try consolidators and hotel-room discounters. You won't hear the same rates twice. On the spot, make a reservation as soon as you are quoted a price you want to pay.

PROMISES, PROMISES If you have special requests, make them when you reserve. Get written confirmation of any promises.

SETTLE IN Upon arriving, make sure everything works—lights and lamps, TV and radio, sink, tub, shower, and anything else that matters. Report any problems immediately. And don't wait until you need extra pillows or blankets or an ironing board to call housekeeping. Also check out the fire emergency instructions. Know where to find the fire exits, and make sure your companions do, too.

IF YOU NEED TO COMPLAIN Be polite but firm. Explain the problem to the person in charge. Suggest a course of action. If you aren't satisfied, repeat your requests to the manager. Document everything: Take pictures and keep a written record of who you've spoken with, when, and what was said. Contact your travel agent, if he made the reservations.

KNOW THE SCORE When you go out, take your hotel's business cards (one for everyone in your party). If you have extras, you can give them out to new acquaintances who want to call you.

TIP UP FRONT For special services, a tip or partial tip in advance can work wonders.

USE ALL THE HOTEL RESOURCES A concierge can make difficult things easy. But a desk clerk, bellhop, or other hotel employee who's friendly, smart, and ambitious can often steer you straight as well. A gratuity is in order if the advice is helpful.

In This Chapter

Updated by Karla Brunet

side trips

SEVERAL DESTINATIONS JUST OUTSIDE São Paulo are perfect for short getaways. Embu's weekend crafts fair and many furniture stores are famous. Although paulistanos often come for a weekend, you can see all the sights in an afternoon. Northwest of the city, water flows in abundance. Soak up the healing properties at the spas and springs of Águas de São Pedro. In Brotas you can go white-water rafting or hike past waterfalls. If you like mountains, try Campos de Jordão; its cafés and clothing stores are often crowded with oh-so-chic paulistanos. For beach lovers, Ilhabela is off the coast from São Sebastião, on the state's North Shore. The island is part of the Mata Atlântica (Atlantic Rain Forest) and is known for its many waterfalls, trails, and diving spots.

EMBU

27 km (17 mi) west of São Paulo.

Embu is a Portuguese colonial town of whitewashed houses, old churches, wood-carvers' studios, and antiques shops. A huge downtown handicrafts fair is held every Saturday and Sunday (on Sunday the streets are so crowded you can barely walk). Embu also has many stores that sell handicrafts and wooden furniture; most of these are close to where the street fair takes place.

The baroque **IGREJA NOSSA SENHORA DO ROSÁRIO** was built in the 18th century. The church contains many images of saints as well as a museum of sacred art. *Largo dos Jesuítas 67, tel. 011/ 494–5333. Free. Tues.–Sun.*

são paulo state

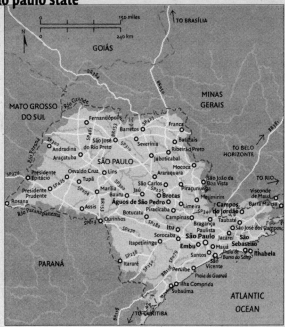

🐝 In the Mata Atlântica you can visit the **CIDADE DAS ABELHAS** (City of the Bees), a bee farm with a small museum. You can buy honey while your kids climb the gigantic model of a bee. It's about 10 minutes from downtown; just follow the signs. *Estrada da Ressaca 9, tel. 011/493–6460. R$3. Tues.–Sun. 8–6.*

Dining

$–$$$$ CELAS. Pull up one of the wooden chairs and prepare to feast on the food of either Minas Gerais or Bahia. *Largo 21 de Abril 75, tel. 011/494–5791. No credit cards.*

$–$$ OS GIRASSÓIS RESTAURANTE E CHOPERIA. Right downtown, this restaurant serves a great variety of dishes, including the recommended *picanha brasileira* (barbecued steak with french fries and manioc flour.) *Rua Nossa Senhora do Rosário 3, tel. 011/4781–2247. AE, DC, MC, V.*

$ CHURRASCARIA GAÚCHA. This roadside barbecue place is inspired by the *churrascarias* of Brazil's south. If meat isn't your thing, check out the large all-you-can-eat salad bar. *Via Régis Bittencourt, Km 280, tel. 011/494–2961. AE, DC, MC, V.*

Shopping

ATELIER LUSTRES MEDIEVAL (Largo 21 de Abril 183, tel. 011/494–2903) specializes in decorator light fixtures. The place is 25 years old and has different kinds of table lamps, floor lamps, and ceiling lamps.

CANTÃO MÓVEIS E GALERIA (Largo dos Jesuítas 169, tel. 011/4781–2247) is a good place to buy ceramics, colonial-style furniture, and antique decorations.

CHOUPANA MÓVEIS RÚSTICOS (Av. Elias Yazbek 2800, tel. 011/494–6177) is one of the biggest places to buy furniture in town. The store makes the items it sells.

CIGANA MÓVEIS RÚSTICOS (Rua Joaquim Santana 16, tel. 011/494–3501) manufactures some of the furniture, curtains, and cushions it sells.

FENIX GALERIA DE ARTES (Rua Marechal Isidoro Lopes 10, tel. 011/494–5634) is a good place to find oil paintings and wood and stone sculptures.

GALERIA JOZAN (Rua Nossa Senhora do Rosarío 59, tel. 011/494–2600) sells unmounted Brazilian gemstones, such as *ametistas* (amethysts) and crystals, which you can have set as you wish.

GUARANI ARTESANATO (Largo dos Jesuítas 153, tel. 011/494–3200) sells handicrafts made of wood and stone, including sculptures carved from pau-brasil.

ÁGUAS DE SÃO PEDRO

190 km (119 mi) northwest of São Paulo.

Sulfurous waters have made Águas de São Pedro famous countrywide. The healing hot springs were discovered by chance in the 1920s when technicians were drilling for oil. Fonte Junventude is the richest in sulfur and is often used to treat rheumatism, asthma, bronchitis, and skin ailments. The waters at Fonte Gioconda have minor radioactive elements (and yes, they are reportedly good for you). And the Fonte Almeida Salle's water has chlorine bicarbonate and sodium in it, which is said to alleviate the symptoms of diabetes and upset stomachs.

You can access the springs at the *balneário publico* (public bathhouse) or through your hotel. You can pay to use hotel facilities whether or not you are staying there. Though a number of illnesses respond to the water, most visitors are just healthy tourists soaking in relaxation. Every July, classical music and song fill the air during the Festival de Julho.

A walk through the woods in **BOSQUE MUNICIPAL DR. OCTÁVIO MOURA ANDRADE** (Av. Carlos Mauro) is a chance to relax. Horseback riding costs R$10 for a half hour.

The **TORRE DE PETRÓLEO ENGENHEIRO ANGELO BALLONI** (Av. Joaquim de Moura Andrade) commemorates the discovery of the town's springs. The tower marks the spot where the city began.

Built in the Swiss style, **CAPELA NOSSA SENHORA APARECIDAB** (Rua Izaura de Algodoal Mauro, Jardim Porangaba) perches atop the highest part of the city. Twelve pine trees were planted around this chapel to represent the Twelve Apostles.

BALNEÁRIO MUNICIPAL DR. OCTÁVIO MOURA ANDRADE (Av. Carlos Mauro, tel. 019/482–1333) offers immersion baths in sulfurous springwater. You can swim in the pool or sweat in the sauna while you wait for your private soak, massage, or beauty appointment. A snack bar and a gift shop round out the spa services.

Dining and Lodging

$–$$$ BIER HAUS. Formerly just a pub, this is now the most popular restaurant in town. People flock in for the pizza and live music. For something more sophisticated, try *peixe na telha*, fish cooked on a ceramic tile. *Av. Carlos Mauro 300, tel. 019/482–1445. DC, MC, V. Closed Mon.–Wed.*

$–$$ RESTAURANTE AVENIDA. This simple restaurant offers tasty home cooking like the *filé Cubana* (steak with fried banana and pineapple), served with rice, vegetables, and french fries. The plastic chairs, along with the rest of the decor, leave something to be desired. *Av. Carlos Mauro 246, tel. 019/482–1422. No credit cards. Closed Mon.*

¢ ZULEICA DOCES. Good coffee and very sweet desserts are found here. Indulge in the *bombom de maracujá trufado* (a chocolate ball with passion-fruit filling). *Av. Carlos Mauro 388, Loja 11, no phone. No credit cards.*

$$–$$$ GRANDE HOTEL SÃO PEDRO. In the 1940s this place was a casino. Nowadays it's a teaching hotel with all the comforts of a full-service spa. Many of the friendly, helpful staff members are students. Rest by the pool, have a massage, or a soak in the sulfurous waters. *Parque Dr. Octavio de Moura Andrade, tel. 019/482–1211, fax 019/482–1665, www.sp.senac.br/ghp. 96 rooms, 16 suites. 2 restaurants, bar, room service, heated pool, hair salon, massage, sauna,* tennis court, exercise room, recreation room, business services, meeting room. AE, DC, MC, V.

$ HOTEL JERUBIAÇABA. Recently updated, the rooms in this 30-year-old hotel are bathed in light colors and filled with simple furnishings. Spa services are offered, or you can float along in the regular swimming pool. *Av. Carlos Mauro 168, tel. 019/482–1411, www.jerubiacaba.com.br. 120 rooms, 8 suites. Restaurant, bar, room service, heated pool, hair salon, massage, tennis court, recreation room, business services, meeting room. AE, DC, MC, V.*

¢ HOTEL AVENIDA. Guests relax on the arcaded veranda of this hotel that resembles a large ranch house. Rooms are plain but spacious. *Av. Carlos Mauro 246, tel. 019/482–1221, fax 019/482–1224. 53 rooms. Restaurant, room service, pool. No credit cards.*

Shopping

ARTE BRASIL (Av. Carlos Mauro 348, tel. 019/482–1260) sells gemstones, willow baskets, and wood ornaments. **ELDORADO** (Av. Carlos Mauro 341, tel. 019/482–1756) sells homemade sweets and liqueurs. The owners are very friendly and will give you a taste of the liqueur before you buy. Try the *doce de leite* (a spongy pudding), a typical Brazilian sweet.

BROTAS

50 km (31 mi) from Águas de São Pedro, 242 km (151 mi) northwest of São Paulo.

No one is sure how the city of Brotas got its name. One theory is that its founder, Dona Francisca Ribeiro dos Reis, a Portuguese woman who was a devout Catholic, dedicated the site to her patron saint, Nossa Senhora das Brotas. Other people think the name originated in the abundant water springing from the landscape. (The verb *brotar* means "to sprout.") The region has approximately 30 *cachoeiras* (waterfalls), many rivers, and endless opportunities for outdoor diversion. Jacaré-Pepira is the main river, which crosses town from east to west. Nearby rafting, canyoning (rappelling down a waterfall), cascading (sliding down waterfalls), rappelling, biking, hiking, and *bóia cross* (floating down the river in an inner tube) are available.

Most visitors use Brotas as a base and branch out with an arranged agency tour. Admission to some of the sights is free; if not, the fee is included in the price of a tour. Insect repellent is essential, especially on afternoon river excursions.

See both artwork and performances at the **CENTRO CULTURAL** (Av. Mário Pinotti 584, tel./fax 014/653–1107 Ext. 233). This 19th-century house used to be a meeting place for the rich and famous.

Seventeen waterfalls are accessible and open to visitors. The **CACHOEIRA ÁGUA BRANCA** is on D. Calila Ranch, 22 km (14 mi) from town; ask for directions. Relax and bathe in the fall's collection pool. On-site is a small distillery were you can try the homemade liqueur. Like everything else in Brazil, it is crowded during summer (January and February).

An hour's walk in the beautiful native forest filled with *jequitibas* and *figueiras* (typical regional trees) brings you to one of the highest waterfalls, the 57-m (186-ft) **CACHOEIRA SANTA MARIA** (Bairro Pinheiro neighborhood, tel. 014/973–6612). The site is 12 km (7.5 mi) from downtown Brotas.

At **CACHOEIRA TRÊS QUEDAS** (Alto de Serra neighborhood, 22 km/14 mi from downtown Brotas, tel. 014/973–6612) you can take a short walk to Cachoeira das Andorinhas for a waterfall shower, then follow the trail to Cachoeira da Figueira, a 40-m (131-ft) waterfall. On the way back stop at the smaller Cachoeirinha das Nascentes to bathe in a collection pool.

CACHOEIRA BELA VISTA (Alto da Serra neighborhood, 28 km/17 mi from downtown Brotas, tel. 014/978–3855) is one of three waterfalls formed by small streams. The Cachoeira Bela Vista and Cachoeira dos Coqueiros are easy to get to, but a longer trek is necessary to reach the Cachoeira dos Macacos. If you are lucky you may see *macacos* (monkeys) on the way.

On the Beneditos ranch, **CACHOEIRA DO ESCORREGADOR** (Alto da Serra, 38 km/23 mi from downtown Brotas, tel. 014/ 978–3855) can be reached by driving toward São Pedro city. The waterfall's natural pools are perfect for cooling off after a light hike. Camping and picnic spots are available, or stop at the snack bar for refreshment.

Dining and Lodging

$ RESTAURANTE CASINHA. A lake view adds ambience to this family-owned restaurant. Try the delicious *pintado na brasa*, a charcoal-grilled fish made with garlic, onions, and lemon. *Av. Lorival Jaubert Braga 1875, tel. 014/653–1225. No credit cards. Closed Mon.–Wed.*

¢–$ MALAGUETA. Owned by a young couple from São Paulo, Malagueta serves grilled meat, salads, and sandwiches. A green and red color scheme gives the place a happy, modern look. *Salada portofino* (lettuce, sun-dried tomatoes, mozzarella, olives, and mustard dressing) is a noteworthy choice. *Av. Mário Pinotti 243, tel. 014/653–2297. No credit cards. Closed Mon.*

¢–$ HOTEL ESTALAGEM QUINTA DAS CACHOEIRAS. Considered the best place in town, this Victorian-style hotel has a staff that prides itself on providing personal attention to their adult guests; no children allowed. *Rua João Rebecca, 225 Parque dos Saltos, tel. 014/ 653–2497. 13 rooms. Air-conditioning, refrigerator, pool, sauna, recreation room. V.*

¢ POUSADA CAMINHO DAS ÁGUAS. The owners of the small inn live on-site, providing a friendly place to rest—and a good breakfast. Rooms are decorated in light colors, with cool ceramic-tile floors. *Av. Mário Pinotti 1110, 13309-010, tel. 014/653–2428. 18 rooms. Fans, refrigerator, pool. No credit cards.*

Outdoor Activities and Sports ....

White-water rafting on the Jacaré-Pepira River is best from November to May. The 9-km (5½-mi) course ranges in difficulty from Class III to Class IV rapids, with drops from 1 to 3 m (3 to 10 ft).

MATA'DENTRO ECOTURISMO E AVENTURA (Av. Mário Pinotti 230, tel. 014/653–1915, www.matadentro.com.br) is the oldest rafting operator in town. It also offers canyoning, rappelling, and hiking excursions. An hour of rafting is about R$48.

You can change in the **VIAS NATURAIS** (Rua João Rebecca 195, tel. 014/653–1855 or 014/653–4050, www.viasnaturais.com.br) dressing rooms—or buy a souvenir at the gift shop—before heading out on a river tour. Horseback riding, hiking, and canyoning are also available.

CAMPOS DO JORDÃO
184 km (114 mi) northeast of São Paulo.

Set in the Serra da Mantiqueira at an altitude of 1,690 m (5,576 ft), Campos do Jordão and its fresh mountain air have attracted visitors for years. In July the temperatures drop as low as 32°F (0°C), though it never snows; in warmer months, temperatures linger in the 13°C–16°C (55°F–60°F) range. Some people come for their health (the town was once a tuberculosis treatment area), others for inspiration, including such Brazilian artists as writer Monteiro Lobato, dramatist Nelson Rodrigues, and painter Lasar Segall. The arts continue to thrive, especially during July's Festival de Inverno (Winter Festival), which draws classical musicians from around the world.

BOULEVARD GENÉVE, in the busy Vila Capivari district, is lined with cafés, bars, and restaurants, making it a nightlife hub. You'll also find many candy shops (many featuring chocolate) and clothing stores.

PALÁCIO BOA VISTA (Rua Dr. Adhemar de Barros 300, tel. 012/262–1122), the official winter residence of the state's governor, has paintings by such famous Brazilian artists as Di Cavalcanti, Portinari, Volpi Tarsila do Amaral, and Malfatti. The associated **Capela de São Pedro** (São Pedro Chapel) has sacred art from the 17th and 18th centuries. Admission is free.

The **HORTO FLORESTAL** (Av. Pedro Paulo, tel. 012/263–1977) is a natural playground for *macacos-prego* (nail monkeys), squirrels, and parrots, as well as people. The park has a trout-filled river, waterfalls, and trails all set among trees from around the world.

Outside town, a chair-lift ride to the top of **MORRO DO ELEFANTE** (Elephant Mountain) is a good way to enjoy the view. The athletically inclined can climb the 370-step iron staircase to the **PEDRA DO BAÚ** (Trunk Stone), north of the city. A trail starts in São Bento de Sapucaí.

Dining and Lodging

$$–$$$ **BADEN-BADEN.** One of the specialties at this charming German restaurant in the heart of town is fondue *misto* (with a variety of meats). *Rua Djalma Forjaz 93, Vila Capivari, tel. 012/263–3610. AE, MC, V.*

$–$$ **ITÁLIA CANTINA E RISTORANTE.** As its name suggests, this place specializes in Italian food. The pasta and the meat dishes are delicious. *Av. Macedo Soares 306, Capivari, tel. 012/263–1140. AE, DC, MC, V.*

$–$$ **SABOR CAFÉ.** This pleasant place serves an all-you-can-eat sequence of fondues: cheese, meat, and, for dessert, chocolate. *Rua Djalma Forjaz 100, Loja 15, Capivari, tel. 012/263–3043. AE, DC, MC, V.*

$$ **POUSADA VILA CAPIVARY.** A stay at this cozy guest house puts you in the gastronomic and commercial center of Campos. The friendly staff is helpful and efficient. *Av. Victor Godinho 131, Vila Capivari 12460-000, tel. 012/263–1746, fax 012/263–1736, www.capivari.com.br. 10 rooms, 5 suites. Hot tub. AE, DC, MC, V.*

$–$$ LAUSANNE HOTEL. Set on an enormous green 7 km (4½ mi) outside town, this hotel offers plenty of solitude and the chance to commune with nature. *Rodovia SP 50, Km 176, Vila Santa Cruz 12460-000, tel. 012/262–2900, fax 011/262–2985. 26 rooms. Restaurant, bar, air-conditioning, pool, tennis court, game room. DC, MC, V.*

Shopping

CASA DE CHOCOLATES MONTANHÊS (Av. Macedo Soares 123, Loja 08, Capivari, tel. 012/263–3205) is a well-known chocolate shop. **GELÉIA DOS MONGES** (Rua Tadeu Rangel Pestana 506, no phone) sells delicious jellies. You'll find handmade embroidered clothing at **GENEVE STORE** (Rua Djalma Forjaz 100, Lojas 01 and 03, Capivari, tel. 012/263–2520). For knit items, try **PALOMA MALHAS** (Rua Djalma Forjaz 78, Loja 11, Capivari, tel. 012/263–1218).

ILHABELA

São Sebastião is 210 km (130 mi) southeast of São Paulo; Ilhabela is 7 km (4½ mi)—a 15-min boat ride—from São Sebastião.

Ilhabela is favored by those who like the beach and water sports; indeed, many championship competitions are held here. Beaches along the western shore are calm. The hotels are mostly at the north end, though the best sandy stretches are to the south. Scuba divers have six wrecks to explore, and hikers will appreciate the abundance of inland trails that often lead to a waterfall (the island has more than 300 of them). Note that mosquitoes are a problem; bring plenty of insect repellent.

There are two small towns on the island: one is where the locals live; the other is where most visitors stay because of its hotels, restaurants, and stores. Most businesses that cater to tourists—including restaurants—are open only on weekends during the winter months.

The best way to get around Ilhabela is by car, which you must rent on the mainland. The ferry from São Sebastião transports vehicles as well as passengers to the island.

PRAIA GRANDE is 6 km (4 mi) south of the ferry dock and has a long sandy strip with food kiosks, a soccer field, and a small church. At night, people gather 6 km (4 mi) south of Praia Grande at **PRAIA DO CURRAL,** where there are many restaurants and bars—some with live music—as well as places to camp. The ship *Aymoré* is sunk off the coast of this beach, near the Ponta do Ribeirão.

A small church and many fishing boats add to the charm of **PRAIA DA ARMAÇÃO,** 14 km (9 mi) north of the ferry dock. The beach was once the place for processing whales caught in the waters around the island. Today, windsurfers stick to capturing the wind and the waves.

To reach **BAÍA DOS CASTELHANOS,** 22 km (14 mi) east of the ferry dock, you need a four-wheel-drive vehicle; if it rains, even this won't be enough. Consider arriving by sailboat, a trip of 1½– 3 hours that can be arranged through local tour operators. With such an isolated location, you can see why slave ships once used the bay to unload their illicit cargo after slavery was banned in Brazil. If you're lucky, you might spot a dolphin.

Dining and Lodging

$–$$$ **VIANA.** This restaurant serves *camarão* (shrimp) prepared in
★ sundry ways, as well as grilled fish. Reservations are recommended; there are only a few tables. *Av. Leonardo Reale 1560, tel. 012/472– 1089. AE, DC, MC, V. Closed Mon.–Thurs. Mar.–June and Aug.–Nov.*

$–$$ **ILHA SUL.** The best option on the menu is the grilled shrimp with vegetables. Fish and other seafood are also available. *Av. Riachuelo 287, tel. 012/472–9426. AE, DC, MC, V. Closed Mon.–Thurs. Mar.–June and Aug.–Nov.*

$–$$$ MAISON JOLY. On arrival, you're given a beach kit complete with
★ mosquito repellent and a hat. Each room is equipped with
something that gives it a theme, such as a piano, a billiard table,
or a telescope. *Rua Antônio Lisboa Alves 278, Morro do Cantagalo, tel.
012/472–1201, fax 012/472–2364, www.maisonjoly.com.br. 10 rooms.
Restaurant, bar, air-conditioning, in-room safes, pool. AE, DC, MC, V.*

¢ POUSADA DOS HIBISCOS. North of the ferry dock, this red house
★ offers midsize air-conditioned rooms. The friendly staff serves up
a good breakfast and provides poolside bar service. *Av. Pedro de
Paula Moraes 714, tel./fax 012/472–1375. 13 rooms. Bar, air-conditioning,
refrigerator, pool, sauna. DC, MC.*

Outdoor Activities and Sports

BOATING AND SAILING
Because of its excellent winds and currents, Ilhabela is a sailor's
mecca. You can arrange boating and sailing trips through
MAREMAR TURISMO (Av. Princesa Isabel 90, Ilhabela, tel. 012/
472–1418), one of the biggest tour agencies in Ilhabela. They
also offer sailing courses.

For information on annual boating competitions that Ilhabela
hosts, including a large Sailing Week, contact the **IATE CLUB DE
ILHABELA** (Av. Força Expedicionária Brasileira 299, tel. 012/472–
2300). If you'd like to learn to sail, **ILHA SAILING OCEAN
SCHOOL** (Av. Pedro de Paula Moraes 578, Hotel da Praia, tel.
012/472–1992) has 12-hour courses that cost roughly R$380.

HIKING
The **CACHOEIRA DOS TRÊS TOMBOS** trail starts at Feiticeira
Beach and leads to three waterfalls. The **TRILHA DA ÁGUA
BRANCA** (Park administration: Rua do Morro da Cruz 608,
Itaguaçú Beach, tel./fax 012/472–2660) is an accessible, well-
marked trail. Three of its paths go to waterfalls that have natural
pools and picnic areas. You can arrange a guided hike through
the park administration.

SCUBA DIVING

Ilhabela has several good dive sites off its shores. In 1894, the British ship **DART** sank near Itaboca, about 17 km (11 mi) south of the ferry dock; it still contains bottles of wine and porcelain dishes. The **ILHA DE BÚZIOS** is a good place to see a variety of marine life. Recommended for beginners is the sanctuary (which has a statue of Neptune at a depth of 22 ft) off the shore of **ILHA DAS CABRAS,** a nearby islet.

You can rent equipment and arrange for a dive-boat trip through **DISCOVER DIVE** (Av. Força Expedicionária Brasileira 147, tel. 012/472–1999).

SURFING

One of the best places to surf is **BAÍA DE CASTELHANOS** (22 km/14 mi east of the ferry dock). **PACUÍBA** offers decent wave action 20 km (12 mi) north of the ferry dock.

The **ASSOCIAÇÃO DE SURF DE ILHABELA** (Rua Espírito Santo 170, Barra Velha, tel. 012/472–8798) promotes surfing events on the island.

WINDSURFING

Savvy windsurfers head to **PONTA DAS CANAS,** at the island's northern tip. **PRAIA DO PINTO AND ARMAÇÃO** (about 12 km/7 mi north of the ferry dock) have favorable wind conditions.

You can take windsurfing and sailing lessons at **BL3** (Engenho D'Água Beach, tel. 012/472–1034; Armação Beach, tel. 012/472–1271), the biggest school in Ilhabela. It costs about R$290 for a 12-hour course.

SIDE TRIPS FROM SÃO PAULO A TO Z

Boat and Ferry Travel

The ferry from São Sebastião to Ilhabela accepts reservations. It's worth making them, particularly from December to February. Ferries run every 20 minutes from 5:30 AM to 1 AM weekdays; weekends see 24-hour service. The fare is R$5 with a car.

➤ INFORMATION: **Ferry** (tel. 0800/55–5510).

Bus Travel

São Pedro buses run daily to Águas de São Pedro from São Paulo's Tietê station. Expresso Prata buses run to Brotas three times a day from São Paulo's Barra Funda station. Viação Litorânea buses leave Tietê station five times daily for the trip to Ilhabela. Viação Mantiqueira buses travel to Campos do Jordão every two hours from Tietê. Every half hour Soamin buses depart for Embu from one of several São Paulo locations.

➤ BUS INFORMATION: **Expresso Prata** (tel. 011/3612–1717). **São Pedro** (tel. 011/6221–0038). **Soamin** (tel. 011/7947–1423). **Viação Litorânea** (tel. 011/6972–0244). **Viação Mantiqueira** (tel. 011/6972–0244).

Car Travel

Roads in São Paulo State are in good condition and are well marked; some of them are toll roads. To make the 30-minute drive from São Paulo to Embu, take Avenida Professor Francisco Morato to the Rodovia Régis Bittencourt and then follow the signs. Águas de São Pedro is about a 2½-hour drive on SP 330, SP 340, and SP 304. Brotas is three hours on SP 330 and SP 340, SP 310, and SP 225. To reach Campos do Jordão from the city (a 2½-hour drive), take the Rodovia Carvalho Pinto and SP 123. The drive from São Paulo to São Sebastião is about 2½ hours; take the Rodovia Ayrton Senna, followed by the Rodovia Tamoios to Caraguatatuba, and then follow the signs.

Emergencies

➤ HOSPITALS AND CLINICS: **Fundação de Saúde** (Rua Antônio Feijó 52, Águas de São Pedro, tel. 019/482–1721). **Pronto Socorro Municipal** (Av. Elias Yazbek 1415, Embu, tel. 011/7822–5744).

Santa Casa (Rua Pe. Bronislau Chereck 15, Ilhabela, tel. 012/
472–1222). **Santa Teresinha** (Av. Rua Barbosa 703, Brotas, tel. 014/
653–1200). **São Paulo** (Rua Agripino Lopes de Morais 1100,
Campos do Jordão, tel. 012/262–1722).

➤ POLICE: (tel. 190).

English-Language Media

Ponto das Letras, in Ilhabela, has a small café-bookstore with
international magazines.

➤ BOOKSTORE: **Ponto das Letras** (Rua Dr. Carvalho 146, tel. 012/
472–2104).

Money Matters

Embu has a branch of Bradesco, as does Águas de São Pedro.
Brotas is served by Banco do Brasil. In Campos do Jordão,
there's an ATM at the Parque Centro Shop; banks include
Bradesco and Itaú. Ilhabela has both Banespa and Bradesco
branches.

➤ BANKS: **Banco do Brasil** (Av. Rodolfo Guimarães 673, Brotas).
Banespa (Rua Dr. Carvalho 98, Ilhabela). **Bradesco** (Praça Cel.
Julião M. Negrão 29 Ilhabela; Rua Boulevard Francisco P. Carneiro
28, Campos; Rua Maranhão 44, Embu; Rua João B. Azevedo, 269,
Águas de São Pedro). **Itaú** (Av. Pelinca 19 Campos).

Tours

As its name suggests, Ilha Tour specializes in tours (by boat,
bike, horse, or jeep) of Ilhabela. Another Ilhabela operator is
Mare Mare, which offers scuba-diving, jeep, horseback-riding,
and hiking tours. HS Turismo offers five tours in or around
Campos do Jordão.

➤ TOUR-OPERATOR RECOMMENDATIONS: **HS Turismo** (Rua Carlina
Antonia Sirin 65, tel. 012/262–2759). **Ilha Tour** (Av. Pedro de Paula

Moraes 149, tel. 012/472–1083). **Mare Mare** (Av. Princesa Isabel 90, tel. 012/472–1418).

Transportation Around Towns Near São Paulo

On weekends, it's difficult to find a place to park in Embu, and parking lots can be expensive. Although you can easily walk to the town's main sights, the *bondinho* (a "train" whose cars are pulled by a truck) crosses Embu and stops at every main square. In Brotas, most natural attractions are outside town, making a car essential. Águas de São Pedro is compact, so it's possible to get around on foot.

Exploring Campos do Jordão without a car is very difficult. The attractions are far-flung, except for those at Vila de Capivari. Trains depart from the Estação Ferroviária Emílio Ribas on tours of the city and its environs (including the 47 km/29 mi trip to Reino das Águas Claras, where there's a park with waterfalls). In Ilhabela a car is the best option, although public buses do cross the island from north to south daily.

➤ CONTACTS: **Estação Ferroviária Emílio Ribas** (tel. 012/263–1531).

Visitor Information

➤ TOURIST INFORMATION: **Embu Secretaria do Turismo** (Largo 21 de Abril 139, tel. 011/494–5333). **Águas de São Pedro Informações Turísticas** (Av. Carlos Mauro, in front of Balneário, tel. 019/482–1811). **Brotas Informações Turísticas–Centro Cultural** (Av. Mário Pinotti 584, tel. 014/653–1107). **Campos do Jordão Tourist Office** (At entrance to town, tel. 012/262–2755). **Ilhabela Secretaria do Turismo** (Rua Bartolomeu de Gusmão 140, tel. 012/472–1091).

practical information

Addresses

In Portuguese *avenida* (avenue) and *travessa* (lane) are abbreviated (as *Av.* and *Trv.* or *Tr.*), while other common terms such as *estrada* (highway) and *rua* (street) often aren't. Street numbers follow the names; postal codes are widely used. In some places street numbering doesn't enjoy the wide popularity it has achieved elsewhere; hence, you may find the notation "s/n," meaning "no street number."

Air Travel

AIRPORTS & TRANSFERS

São Paulo's international airport, Aeroporto Cumbica, is in the suburb of Guarulhos, 30 km (19 mi) and a 45-minute drive (longer during rush hour or on rainy days) northeast of Centro. Aeroporto Congonhas, 14 km (9 mi) south of Centro (a 15- to 30-minute drive, depending on traffic), serves regional airlines, including the Rio–São Paulo shuttle. From June to September, both airports are sometimes fogged in during the early morning, and flights are rerouted to the Aeroporto Viracopos in Campinas; passengers are transported by bus (an hour's ride) to São Paulo.

EMTU *executivo* buses—fancy, green-stripe "executive" vehicles—shuttle between Cumbica and Congonhas (6 AM–10 PM, every 30 mins) as well as between Cumbica and the Tietê bus terminal (5:40 AM–10 PM, every 45 mins); the downtown Praça da República (5:30 AM–11 PM, every 30 mins); and the Hotel

Maksoud Plaza (6:45 AM–11 PM every 35 mins), stopping at most major hotels on Avenida Paulista. The cost is R$12. Municipal buses, with CMTC painted on the side, stop at the airport and go downtown by various routes, such as via Avenida Paulista, to the Praça da Sé and the Tietê bus station.

The sleek, blue-and-white, air-conditioned Guarucoop radio taxis will take you from Cumbica to downtown for around R$45; the fare to town from Congonhas is about R$20. Comum (regular) taxis also charge R$40 from Cumbica and around R$18 from Congonhas. Fleet Car Shuttle (counter at Cumbica Airport's arrivals Terminal 1) is open daily 6 AM–midnight, and serves groups of up to 10 people in a van, stopping at one destination of choice. The fee (for the vanload) is about R$70.

➤ **AIRPORT INFORMATION: Aeroporto Congonhas** (tel. 011/5090–9000). **Aeroporto Cumbica** (tel. 011/6445–2945). **Aeroporto Viracopos** (tel. 019/725–5000).

➤ **TAXIS AND SHUTTLES: EMTU** *executivo* **buses** (tel. 0800/19–0088). **Fleet Car Shuttle** (tel. 011/945–3030). **Guarucoop radio taxis** (tel. 011/208–1881).

CARRIERS

Aerolíneas Argentinas has daily flights from Buenos Aires and Madrid and twice-a-week service from Auckland, New Zealand, and Sydney, Australia. Air France has a daily flight from Paris. American Airlines offers three flights a day from Miami and one a day from both New York and Dallas. British Airways flies from London every day but Tuesday and Wednesday. Canadian Airlines flies from Toronto every day but Monday. Continental Airlines flies from New York daily; United Airlines flies daily from Miami, New York, and Chicago.

Rio-Sul and Nordeste connect São Paulo with most major Brazilian cities daily. TAM flies daily to Miami, Paris, and most major Brazilian cities. It serves Mercosur capitals as well. Transbrasil has daily flights to major Brazilian cities. Varig has daily service to many U.S. and Brazilian cities; it also offers regular service to more than 18 countries in Latin America, Europe, Asia, and Australia. VASP serves all major Brazilian cities daily. GOL, the youngest Brazilian airline, offers budget tickets to major national capitals.

➤ **BRAZILIAN CARRIERS: GOL** (tel. 0800/70–12131). **Rio-Sul and Nordeste** (tel. 0800/99–2004 or 011/5561–2161). **TAM** (tel. 888/ 235–9826 in the U.S. or 305/406–2826 in Miami). **Transbrasil** (tel. 800/872–3153 in the U.S.). **Varig** (tel. 800/468–2744 in the U.S.). **VASP** (tel. 0800/99–8277).

➤ **NORTH AMERICAN CARRIERS: Air Canada** (tel. 888/247–2262 in North America). **American Airlines** (tel. 800/433–7300 in North America). **Continental Airlines** (tel. 800/231–0856 in North America). **Delta Airlines** (tel. 800/241–4141 in North America). **United Airlines** (tel. 800/241–6522 in North America).

➤ **FROM AUSTRALIA AND NEW ZEALAND: Aerolíneas Argentinas** (tel. 011/6445–3806). **Air New Zealand** (tel. 13–24–76 in Australia; 0800/737–000 in New Zealand). **Qantas** (tel. 13–13–13 in Australia; 357–8900 in Auckland; 0800/808–767 rest of New Zealand).

➤ **FROM THE U.K.: Air France** (tel. 011/3049–0909). **American Airlines** (tel. 0845/778–9789). **British Airways** (tel. 0845/773–3377). **Continental Airlines** (tel. 0800/776–464). **TAM Airlines** (tel. 0207/707–4586). **United Airlines** (tel. 0845/844–4777). **Varig** (tel. 0207/478–2114).

CHECK-IN & BOARDING

Always bring a government-issued photo ID to the airport. You may be asked to show it before you're allowed to check in. Be prepared to show your passport when leaving Brazil and to pay a hefty departure tax, which runs about R$78 ($36) for international flights. A departure tax also applies to flights within Brazil. Although the amount varies, figure on R$11–R$22 ($5–$10). Although some airports accept credit cards as payment for departure taxes, it's wise to have the appropriate amount in reais.

FLYING TIMES

The flying time is 9½ hours from New York, eight hours from Miami, and 13 hours from Los Angeles. From London, it's seven hours to São Paulo.

Within Brazil, it's one hour to Rio, four hours to Manaus, and 1½ hours to Iguaçu Falls.

RECONFIRMING

Always **reconfirm your flights**, even if you have a ticket and a reservation. This is particularly true for travel within Brazil and throughout South America, where flights tend to operate at full capacity—usually with passengers who have a great deal of baggage to process before departure.

Bus Travel To and From São Paolo

The huge main station—serving all major Brazilian cities (with trips to Rio every hour on the half hour) as well as Argentina, Uruguay, Chile, and Paraguay—is the Terminal Tietê in the north, on the Marginal Tietê Beltway. Terminal Bresser, in the eastern district of Brás, serves southern Minas Gerais State and Belo Horizonte. Terminal Jabaquara, near Congonhas Airport, serves coastal towns. Terminal Barra Funda, in the west, near the Memorial da América Latina, has buses to and from western Brazil. All stations have or are close to metrô stops. You can buy tickets at the stations; although those for Rio de Janeiro can be bought a few minutes before departure, it's best to buy tickets in advance for other destinations and during holiday seasons.

Lengthy bus trips anywhere will involve travel over some bad highways, an unfortunate fact of life in Brazil today. Trips to northern, northeastern, and central Brazil tend to be especially trying; the best paved highways are in the south and southeast, so trips to and within this region may go more smoothly. When traveling by bus, **bring water, toilet paper, and an additional top layer of clothing** (the latter will come in handy if it gets cold, or it can serve as a pillow). Travel light, dress comfortably, and **keep a close watch on your belongings**—especially in bus stations.

➤ **BUS INFORMATION: Bus stations** (tel. 011/235–0322 for information on all stations). **Terminal Barra Funda** (Rua Mário de Andrade 664, Barra Funda). **Terminal Bresser** (Rua do Hipódromo, Brás). **Terminal Jabaquara** (Rua Jequitibas, Jabaquara). **Terminal Tietê** (Av. Cruzeiro do Sul, Santana).

Bus Travel Within São Paolo

There's ample municipal bus service, but regular buses (white with a red horizontal stripe) are overcrowded at rush hour and when it rains. Stops are clearly marked, but routes are spelled out only on the buses themselves. To get a bus to stop, put out your arm horizontally. The fare is R$1.15. You enter at the front, pay the *cobrador* (fare collector) in the middle, and exit at the back. The cobrador gives out *vale transporte* slips, or fare vouchers (with no expiration time), and often has no change.

The green-and-gray SPTrans executivo buses, whose numerical designations all end with the letter E, are more spacious and cost around R$2 (you pay the driver upon entry). Many *clandestino* buses (unlicensed, privately run) traverse the city. Although not very pleasing to the eye—most are battered white vehicles that have no signs—it's perfectly fine to take them; they charge the same as SPTrans buses.

For bus numbers and names, routes, and schedules for SPTrans buses, purchase the *Guia São Paulo Ruas*, published by Quatro Rodas and sold at newsstands and bookstores for about R$30.

➤ **BUS INFORMATION: Municipal bus service** (tel. 0800/12–3133 transit information). **SPTrans executivo** (tel. 158).

Business Hours

BANKS & OFFICES

Banks are, with a few exceptions, open weekdays 10–4. Office hours are generally 9–5.

GAS STATIONS
Within cities and along major highways, many gas stations are open 24 hours a day, seven days a week.

MUSEUMS
Many museums are open from 10 or 11 to 5 or 6 (they may stay open later one night a week). Some museums, however, are open only in the afternoon, and many are closed on Monday. Always check ahead.

SHOPS
Generally, small shops are open weekdays from 9 to 6 and on Saturday from 9 to 1 or 2. Centers and malls are often open from 10 to 10. Some centers, malls, and pharmacies are open on Sunday.

Car Rental

Car-rental rates range from R$60 to R$100 a day. Major rental companies include Avis, Hertz, and Localiza.

Always give the rental car a once-over to make sure the headlights, jack, and tires (including the spare) are in working condition.

➤ **MAJOR AGENCIES: Avis** (Rua da Consolação 335, Centro, tel. 0800/55–0066). **Hertz** (Rua da Consolação 439, Centro, tel. 011/ 258–8422).

➤ **LOCAL AGENCY: Localiza** (Rua da Consolação 419, Centro, tel. 0800/99–2000).

INSURANCE
When driving a rented car you are generally responsible for any damage to or loss of the vehicle as well as for any property damage or personal injury that you may cause. Before you rent, see what coverage your personal auto-insurance policy and credit cards provide.

REQUIREMENTS & RESTRICTIONS

In Brazil, the minimum driving age is 18. Your own driver's license is acceptable—sort of. An international driver's license, available from automobile associations, is a *really* good idea. If you do plan to drive in Brazil, find out in advance from a car rental agency what type of proof of insurance you need to carry.

SURCHARGES

Before you pick up a car in one city and leave it in another, **ask about drop-off charges or one-way service fees,** which can be substantial. Note, too, that some rental agencies charge extra if you return the car before the time specified in your contract. To avoid a hefty refueling fee, **fill the tank just before you turn in the car,** but be aware that gas stations near the rental outlet may overcharge.

Car Travel

The main São Paulo–Rio de Janeiro highway is the Via Dutra (BR 116 North), which has been repaved and enlarged in places. The speed limit is 120 kph (74 mph) along most of it, and although it has many tolls, you'll find many call boxes you can use if your car breaks down. The modern Rodovia Ayrton Senna (SP 70) charges reasonable tolls, runs parallel to the Dutra for about a quarter of the way, and is an excellent alternative route. The 429-km (279-mi) trip takes five hours. If you have time, consider the longer, spectacular coastal Rio–Santos Highway (SP 55 and BR 101). It's an easy two-day drive, and you can stop midway at the colonial city of Parati, in Rio de Janeiro State.

Other main highways are the Castelo Branco (SP 280), which links the southwestern part of the state to the city; the Via Anhanguera (SP 330), which originates in the state's rich northern agricultural region, passing through the university town of Campinas; SP 310, which also runs from the farming heartland; BR 116 south, which comes up from Curitiba (a 408 km/265 mi trip); plus the Via Anchieta (SP 150) and the Rodovia Imigrantes (SP 160), parallel roads that run to the coast, each operating one-way on weekends and holidays.

Driving isn't recommended because of the heavy traffic (nothing moves at rush hour, especially when it rains), daredevil drivers, and inadequate parking. If, however, you do opt to drive, there are a few things to keep in mind. Most of São Paulo is between the Rio Tietê and the Rio Pinheiros, which converge in the western part of town. The high-speed routes along these rivers are Marginal Tietê and Marginal Pinheiros. There are also *marginais* (beltways) around the city. Avenida 23 de Maio runs south from Centro and beneath the Parque do Ibirapuera via the Ayrton Senna Tunnel. You can take Avenida Paulista, Avenida Brasil, and Avenida Faria Lima southwest to the Morumbi, Brooklin, Itaim, and Santo Amaro neighborhoods. The Elevado Costa e Silva, also called Minhocão, is an elevated road that connects Centro with Avenida Francisco Matarazzo in the west.

In most commercial neighborhoods you must buy hourly tickets (called Cartão Zona Azul) to park on the street during business hours. Only buy them at newsstands, not from people on the street. Booklets of 20 tickets cost R$16. Fill out each ticket—you'll need one for every hour you plan to park—with the car's license plate and the time you initially parked. Leave the tickets in the car's window so they're visible to officials from outside. After business hours or at any time near major sights, people may offer to watch your car. Although paying these "caretakers" about R$3 is enough to keep your car's paint job intact, to truly ensure its safety opt for a parking lot. Rates are R$5–R$7 for the first hour and R$1–R$2 each hour thereafter.

EMERGENCY SERVICES

The Automóvel Clube do Brasil (Automobile Club of Brazil) provides emergency assistance to foreign motorists in cities and on highways, but only if they're members of an automobile club in their own nation.

➤ **CONTACT: Automóvel Clube do Brasil** (Rua do Passeio 90, Rio de Janeiro tel. 021/2240–4060 or 021/2240–4191).

GASOLINE

Gasoline in Brazil costs around R$1.90 (88¢) a liter. Unleaded gas, called *especial*, costs about the same. Brazil also has an extensive fleet of ethanol-powered cars. Ethanol fuel is sold at all gas stations and is priced a little less than gasoline. However, such cars get lower mileage, so they offer little advantage over gas-powered cars. Stations are plentiful both within cities and on major highways, and many are open 24 hours a day. In smaller towns, few stations take credit cards, and their hours are more limited.

RULES OF THE ROAD

Brazilians drive on the right, and in general, traffic laws are the same as those in the United States. The use of seat belts is mandatory. The national speed limit is 80 kph (48 mph) but is seldom observed. In theory, foreign driver's licenses are acceptable. In practice, however, police (particularly highway police) have been known to claim that driving with a foreign license is a violation in order to shake down drivers for bribes. It's best to get an international driver's license, which is seldom challenged. If you do get a ticket for some sort of violation—real or imagined—don't argue. And plan to spend longer than you want settling it.

Children in Brazil

Brazilians love children, and having yours along may prove to be your ticket to meeting locals. Children are welcomed in hotels and restaurants, especially on weekends, when Brazilian families go out for brunch or lunch in droves.

Let older children join in on planning as you outline your trip. Scout your library for picture books, story books, and maps about places you'll be going. Try to explain the concept of foreign language; some kids, who may have just learned to talk, are thrown when they can't understand strangers and strangers can't understand them. On sightseeing days try to **schedule activities of special interest to your children.** If you are renting a car, don't forget to **arrange for a car seat** when you reserve. For general advice about traveling with children, check out *Fodor's FYI: Travel with Your Baby* (available in bookstores everywhere).

LODGING
Many hotels in Brazil allow children under a certain age to stay in their parents' room at no extra charge. Others charge for them as extra adults; be sure to **find out the cutoff age for children's discounts.**

PRECAUTIONS
Any person under the age of 18 who isn't traveling with both parents or legal guardian(s) must provide a notarized letter of consent signed by the nonaccompanying parent or guardian. The notarized letter must be authenticated by the Brazilian embassy or consulate and translated into Portuguese.

Children must have all their inoculations up to date (those between the ages of three months and six years must have an international polio vaccination certificate) before leaving home.

SIGHTS & ATTRACTIONS
Places that are especially appealing to children are indicated by a rubber-duckie icon (☺) in the margin.

SUPPLIES & EQUIPMENT
Pack things to keep your children busy while traveling. For children of reading age, **bring books from home;** locally, literature for kids in English is hard to find. Inexpensive art supplies such as crayons (*giz de cera*), paint (*tinta*), and coloring books (*livros de pintar*) are sold in stationery stores, bookstores, newsstands, and some supermarkets and street stalls.

You'll find international brands of baby formula (*leite nan*) and diapers (*fraldas*) in drugstores, supermarkets, and convenience shops. The average cost of a 450-gram (16-ounce) container of formula is R$9 ($4). The average price for a package of diapers is R$9 ($4).

Computers on the Road

If you're traveling with a laptop, carry a spare battery, a universal adapter plug, and a converter if your computer isn't dual voltage. Ask about electrical surges before plugging in your computer. Keep your disks out of the sun and avoid excessive heat for both your computer and disks. In Brazil, carrying a laptop computer signals wealth and could make you a target for thieves; conceal your laptop in a generic bag, and keep it close to you at all times.

Internet access is surprisingly widespread. In addition to business centers in luxury hotels and full-fledged cybercafés, look for computers set up in telephone offices. Rates range from R$6.50 ($3) to R$22 ($10) an hour. Dial-up speeds are variable, though they tend toward the sluggish.

Consulates

➤ **CONTACTS: Australia** (Av. Tenente Negrão 140/121, 12th floor, Itaim Bibi, tel. 011/3849–6281). **Canada** (Av. Paulista 1106, 1st floor, Cerqueira César, tel. 011/5509–4321). **New Zealand** (Rua Pais de Araújo 29, 12th floor, Jardim Europa, tel. 011/3845–5532). **United Kingdom** (Av. Paulista 1938, 17th floor, Cerqueira César, tel. 011/287–7722). **United States** (Rua Padre João Manoel 933, Jardins, tel. 011/3081–6511).

Customs & Duties

When shopping, **keep receipts** for all purchases. Upon reentering the country, **be ready to show customs officials what you've bought.** If you feel a duty is incorrect or object to the way your clearance was handled, note the inspector's badge number and ask to see a supervisor. If the problem isn't resolved, write to the appropriate authorities, beginning with the port director at your point of entry.

IN BRAZIL

Formerly strict import controls have been substantially liberalized as part of the Brazilian government's efforts to open up the nation's economy. In addition to personal items, you're now permitted to bring in, duty-free, up to R$1,085 ($500) worth of gifts purchased abroad, including up to 2 liters of liquor. If you plan to bring in plants, you may do so only with documentation authenticated by the consular service.

IN AUSTRALIA

Australian residents who are 18 or older may bring home $A400 worth of souvenirs and gifts (including jewelry), 250 cigarettes or 250 grams of tobacco, and 1,125 ml of alcohol (including wine, beer, and spirits). Residents under 18 may bring back $A200 worth of goods. Prohibited items include meat products. Seeds, plants, and fruits need to be declared upon arrival.

➤ **INFORMATION: Australian Customs Service** (Regional Director, Box 8, Sydney, NSW 2001, Australia, tel. 02/9213–2000, fax 02/9213–4000, www.customs.gov.au).

IN CANADA

Canadian residents who have been out of Canada for at least seven days may bring home C$500 worth of goods duty-free. If you've been away fewer than seven days but more than 48 hours, the duty-free allowance drops to C$200; if your trip lasts 24–48 hours, the allowance is C$50. You may not pool allowances with family members. Goods claimed under the C$500 exemption may follow you by mail; those claimed under the lesser exemptions must accompany you. Alcohol and tobacco products may be included in the seven-day and 48-hour exemptions but not in the 24-hour exemption. If you meet the age requirements of the province or territory through which you reenter Canada, you may bring in, duty-free, 1.14 liters (40 imperial ounces) of wine or liquor or 24 12-ounce cans or bottles of beer or ale. If you are 16 or older you may bring in, duty-free, 200 cigarettes and 50 cigars. Check ahead of time with Revenue Canada or the Department of Agriculture for policies regarding meat products, seeds, plants, and fruits.

You may send an unlimited number of gifts worth up to C$60 each duty-free to Canada. Label the package UNSOLICITED GIFT— VALUE UNDER $60. Alcohol and tobacco are excluded.

➤ **INFORMATION: Revenue Canada** (2265 St. Laurent Blvd. S, Ottawa, Ontario K1G 4K3, Canada, tel. 613/993–0534; 800/461–9999 in Canada, fax 613/991–4126, www.ccra-adrc.gc.ca).

IN NEW ZEALAND
Homeward-bound residents 17 or older may bring back $700 worth of souvenirs and gifts. Your duty-free allowance also includes 4.5 liters of wine or beer; one 1,125-ml bottle of spirits; and either 200 cigarettes, 250 grams of tobacco, 50 cigars, or a combination of the three up to 250 grams. Prohibited items include meat products, seeds, plants, and fruits.

➤ **INFORMATION: New Zealand Customs** (Custom House, 50 Anzac Ave., Box 29, Auckland, New Zealand, tel. 09/300–5399, fax 09/359–6730, www.customs.govt.nz).

IN THE U.K.
From countries outside the EU, including Brazil, you may bring home, duty-free, 200 cigarettes or 50 cigars; 1 liter of spirits or 2 liters of fortified or sparkling wine or liqueurs; 2 liters of still table wine; 60 ml of perfume; 250 ml of toilet water; plus £136 worth of other goods, including gifts and souvenirs. If returning from outside the EU, prohibited items include meat products, seeds, plants, and fruits.

➤ **INFORMATION: HM Customs and Excise** (St. Christopher House, Southwark, London, SE1 0TE, U.K., tel. 020/7928–3344, tel. 020/7202–4227, www.hmce.gov.uk).

IN THE U.S.

U.S. residents who have been out of the country for at least 48 hours (and who have not used the $400 allowance or any part of it in the past 30 days) may bring home $400 worth of foreign goods duty-free.

U.S. residents 21 and older may bring back 1 liter of alcohol duty-free. In addition, regardless of your age, you are allowed 200 cigarettes and 100 non-Cuban cigars. Antiques, which the U.S. Customs Service defines as objects more than 100 years old, enter duty-free, as do original works of art done entirely by hand, including paintings, drawings, and sculptures.

You may also mail or ship packages home duty-free: up to $200 worth of goods for personal use, with a limit of one parcel per addressee per day (except alcohol or tobacco products or perfume worth more than $5); label the package PERSONAL USE and attach a list of its contents and their retail value. Do not label the package UNSOLICITED GIFT or your duty-free exemption will drop to $100. Mailed items do not affect your duty-free allowance on your return.

➤ **INFORMATION: U.S. Customs Service** (1300 Pennsylvania Ave. NW, Washington, DC 20229, www.customs.gov; inquiries tel. 202/354–1000; complaints c/o 1300 Pennsylvania Ave. NW, Room 5.4D, Washington, DC 20229; registration of equipment c/o Resource Management, tel. 202/927–0540).

Dining

Eating is a national passion, and portions are huge. In many restaurants, plates are prepared for two people; when you order, ask if one plate will suffice. The restaurants (all of which are indicated by an ✗) that we list are the cream of the crop in each price category. Properties indicated by an are lodging establishments whose restaurant warrants a special trip.

MEALTIMES

You'll be hard-pressed to find breakfast outside a hotel restaurant. At lunch and dinner, portions are large. Often a single dish will easily feed two people; no one will be the least surprised if you order one entrée and two plates. In addition, some restaurants automatically bring a *couberto* (an appetizer course of such items as bread, cheese or pâté, olives, quail eggs, and the like). You'll be charged extra for this, and you're perfectly within your rights to send it back if you don't want it.

Mealtimes vary according to locale. In São Paulo, lunch and dinner are served later than in the United States. In restaurants, lunch usually starts around 1 and can last until 3. Dinner is always eaten after 8 and, in many cases, not until 10.

PAYING

Credit cards are widely accepted at restaurants in the major cities. In the countryside, all but the smallest establishments generally accept credit cards as well.

WINE, BEER, & SPIRITS

The national drink is the *caipirinha*, made of crushed lime, sugar, and *pinga* or *cachaça* (sugarcane liquor). When whipped with crushed ice, fruit juices, and condensed milk, the pinga/cachaça becomes a *batida*. A *caipivodka*, or *caipiroska*, is the same cocktail with vodka instead of cachaça. Some bars make both drinks using a fruit other than lime, such as kiwi and *maracujá* (passion fruit). Brazil's best bottled beer is Cerpa, sold at most restaurants. In general, though, Brazilians prefer tap beer, called *chopp*, which is sold by all bars and some restaurants. Be sure to try the carbonated soft drink *guaraná*, made using the Amazonian fruit of the same name.

Disabilities & Accessibility

Although international chain hotels in large cities have some suitable rooms and facilities and it's easy to hire private cars and drivers for excursions, Brazil isn't very well equipped to handle travelers with disabilities. There are few ramps and curb cuts, and it takes effort and planning to negotiate cobbled city streets, get around museums and other buildings, and explore the countryside.

City centers are your best bets. Legislation concerning people with disabilities has been approved but has yet to be enforced. There's no central clearinghouse for information on this topic, so the best local resource is the staff at your hotel.

RESERVATIONS

When discussing accessibility with an operator or reservations agent, **ask hard questions.** Are there any stairs, inside or out? Are there grab bars next to the toilet *and* in the shower/tub? How wide is the doorway to the room? To the bathroom? For the most extensive facilities meeting the latest legal specifications, **opt for newer accommodations.**

Electricity

The current in Brazil isn't regulated: in São Paulo and Rio, it's 110 or 120 volts, 60 cycles alternating current (the same as in the United States and Canada). **Bring a converter.**

Wall outlets take Continental-type plugs, with two round prongs. **Consider buying a universal adapter;** the the Swiss Army knife of adapters, a universal has several types of plugs in one handy unit. If your appliances are dual-voltage (as many laptops are), you'll need only an adapter. Don't use 110-volt outlets, marked FOR SHAVERS ONLY, for high-wattage appliances such as blow-dryers.

Emergencies

The three main pharmacies—Droga Raia, Drogaria São Paulo, and Drogasil—have more than 20 stores, each open 24 hours. The police department in charge of tourist affairs, Delegacia de Turismo, is open weekdays 8–8.

➤ **EMERGENCY SERVICES: Ambulance** (tel. 192). **Delegacia de Turismo** (Av. São Luís 91, Centro, tel. 011/3107–8712). **Fire** (tel. 193). **Police (military)** (tel. 190).

➤ **HOSPITALS: Albert Einstein** (Av. Albert Einstein 627, Morumbi, tel. 011/3745–1233). **Beneficência Portuguesa** (Rua Maestro Cardim 769, Paraíso, tel. 011/253–5022). **Sírio Libanês** (Rua. D. Adma Jafet 91, Bela Vista, tel. 011/3155–0200).

➤ **24-HOUR PHARMACIES: Droga Raia** (Rua José Maria Lisboa 645, Jardim Paulistano, tel. 011/3884–8235). **Drogaria São Paulo** (Av. Angélica 1465, Higienópolis, tel. 011/3667–6291). **Drogasil** (Av. Brigadeiro Faria Lima 2726, Cidade Jardim, tel. 011/3812–6276).

Etiquette & Behavior

Although Brazil is a predominately Catholic country, in many places there's an anything-goes outlook. As a rule, coastal areas (particularly Rio and parts of the northeast) are considerably less conservative than inland areas and those throughout the south. People dress nicely to enter churches, and hats are frowned upon during mass.

Whether they tend toward the conservative or the risqué, Brazilians are a very friendly lot. **Don't be afraid to smile in the streets, ask for directions, or strike up a conversation with a local** (be aware, however, that a Brazilian may give you false directions before admitting that he or she doesn't know where to point you). The slower pace of life in much of the country reflects an unwavering appreciation of family and friendship (as well as a respect for the heat); knowing this will help you understand why things may take a little longer to get done.

Throughout the country, **use the thumbs-up gesture to indicate that something is OK.** The gesture created by making a circle with your thumb and index finger and holding your other fingers up in the air has a very rude meaning.

Gay & Lesbian Travel

Brazil is South America's most popular destination for gay and lesbian travelers, and São Paulo has numerous gay bars, organizations, and publications. Realize, however, that the acceptance of same-sex couples in the major cities may be limited to more touristy areas. Outside these destinations use discretion about public displays of affection.

The great Carnaval celebrations include many gay parades. At the end of the year, Mix Brasil International Festival of Sexual Diversity takes place in São Paulo.

➤ **GAY- & LESBIAN-FRIENDLY TRAVEL AGENCIES: Different Roads Travel** (8383 Wilshire Blvd., Suite 902, Beverly Hills, CA 90211, tel. 323/651–5557 or 800/429–8747, fax 323/651–3678). **Kennedy Travel** (314 Jericho Turnpike, Floral Park, NY 11001, tel. 516/352–4888 or 800/237–7433, fax 516/354–8849, www.kennedytravel.com). **Now Voyager** (4406 18th St., San Francisco, CA 94114, tel. 415/626–1169 or 800/255–6951, fax 415/626–8626, www.nowvoyager.com). **Skylink Travel and Tour** (1006 Mendocino Ave., Santa Rosa, CA 95401, tel. 707/546–9888 or 800/225–5759, fax 707/546–9891, www.skylinktravel.com), serving lesbian travelers.

Health

FOOD & DRINK
Don't drink tap water. Ask for juice and ice made with bottled water in restaurants and bars. **Don't eat barbecued meats sold by street vendors;** even those served in some bars are suspect.

MEDICAL PLANS
No one plans to get sick while traveling, but it happens, so **consider signing up with a medical-assistance company.** Members get doctor referrals, emergency evacuation or repatriation, hot lines for medical consultation, cash for emergencies, and other assistance.

➤ **MEDICAL-ASSISTANCE COMPANIES: International SOS Assistance** (www.internationalsos.com; 8 Neshaminy Interplex, Suite 207, Trevose, PA 19053, tel. 215/245–4707 or 800/523–6586, fax 215/244–9617; 12 Chemin Riantbosson, 1217 Meyrin 1, Geneva, Switzerland, tel. 4122/785–6464, fax 4122/785–6424; 331 N. Bridge Rd., 17-00, Odeon Towers, Singapore 188720, tel. 65/338–7800, fax 65/338–7611).

OVER-THE-COUNTER REMEDIES

Mild cases of diarrhea may respond to Imodium (known generically as loperamide) or Pepto-Bismol (not as strong), both of which can be purchased over the counter. Drink plenty of purified water or *chá* (tea)—*camomila* (chamomile) is a good folk remedy. In severe cases, rehydrate yourself with a salt–sugar solution: ½ teaspoon *sal* (salt) and 4 tablespoons *açúcar* (sugar) per quart of *agua* (water). The word for aspirin is *aspirinha*; Tylenol is pronounced *tee-luh-nawl*.

PESTS & OTHER HAZARDS

The air pollution might irritate your eyes, especially in July and August (dirty air is held in the city by thermal inversions), so **pack eye drops.**

Heatstroke and heat prostration are common though easily preventable maladies. The symptoms for either can vary but always start with headaches, nausea, and dizziness. If ignored, these symptoms can worsen until you require medical attention. In hot weather be sure to **rehydrate regularly, wear loose, lightweight clothing, and avoid overexerting yourself.**

Aside from the obvious safe-sex precautions, keep in mind that Brazil's blood supply isn't subject to the same intense screening as it is in North America, western Europe, Australia, or New Zealand. If you need a transfusion and circumstances permit it, ask that the blood be screened. Insulin-dependent diabetics or those who require injections should pack enough of the appropriate supplies—syringes, needles, disinfectants—to last the trip. In addition, you might want to resist the temptation to get a new tattoo or body piercing while you're in Brazil.

SHOTS & MEDICATIONS

All travelers should have up-to-date tetanus boosters, and a hepatitis A inoculation can prevent one of the most common intestinal infections. If you're heading to tropical regions, you should get yellow fever shots, particularly if you're traveling overland from a country where yellow fever has been prevalent, such as Peru or Bolivia. Children must have current inoculations against measles, mumps, rubella, and polio.

According to the Centers for Disease Control (CDC) there's a limited risk of contracting cholera, typhoid, malaria, hepatitis B, dengue, and chagas. Although a few of these can be contracted anywhere in the country, most cases occur in jungle areas. If you plan to visit remote regions or stay for more than six weeks, **check with the CDC's International Travelers' Hot Line.**

In areas with malaria and dengue, which are both carried by mosquitoes, take mosquito nets, wear clothing that covers the body, apply repellent containing DEET, and use a spray against flying insects in living and sleeping areas.

The hot line recommends chloroquine (analen) as an antimalarial agent. (Note that in parts of northern Brazil, a particularly aggressive strain of malaria has become resistant to chloroquine and may be treated with mefloquine [also known by its trade name Lariam], an expensive alternative that can also have some rather unpleasant side effects—from headaches, nausea, and dizziness to psychosis, convulsions, and hallucinations.)

Dengue has become an increasing problem in the Amazon and Pantanal regions. Unlike malaria, it's primarily a concern in urban areas and is spread by mosquitoes that are more active during the day than at night. No vaccine exists against dengue.

➤ **HEALTH WARNINGS: National Centers for Disease Control and Prevention** (CDC; National Center for Infectious Diseases, Division of Quarantine, Traveler's Health Section, 1600 Clifton Rd. NE, M/S E-03, Atlanta, GA 30333, tel. 888/232–3228 or 800/311–3435, fax 888/232–3299, www.cdc.gov).

Holidays

Major national holidays include: New Year's Day (Jan. 1); Epiphany (Jan. 6); Carnaval, the week preceding Ash Wednesday (which falls on Feb. 13 in 2002 and Mar. 5 in 2003); Good Friday (Mar. 29, 2002; Apr. 18, 2003); Easter (Mar. 31, 2002; Apr. 20, 2003); Tiradentes Day (Apr. 21); Labor Day (May 1); Corpus Christi (May 30, 2002; June 9, 2003); Independence Day (Sept. 7); Our Lady of Aparecida Day (Oct. 12); All Souls' Day (Nov. 1); Declaration of the Republic Day (Nov. 15); Christmas (Dec. 25).

Language

The language in Brazil is Portuguese, not Spanish, and Brazilians will appreciate it if you know the difference. The two languages are distinct, but common origins mean that many words are similar, and fluent speakers of Spanish will be able to make themselves understood. English is spoken among educated Brazilians and, in general, by at least some of the staff at hotels, tour operators, and travel agencies. Store clerks and waiters may have a smattering of English; taxi and bus drivers won't. As in many places throughout the world, you're more likely to find English-speaking locals in major cities than in small towns or the countryside. (Note that in the northeast you may even have difficulty in the cities.)

Lodging

When you consider your lodgings in Brazil, add these three terms to your vocabulary: *pousada* (inn), *fazenda* (farm), and "flat" or "block" hotel (apartment-hotel). Flat hotels are popular with Brazilians, particularly in cities and with families and groups. Some have amenities such as pools, but for most folks, the biggest draw is affordability: with kitchen facilities and room for a group, flat hotels offer more for the money.

If you ask for a double room, you'll get a room for two people, but you're not guaranteed a double mattress. If you'd like to avoid twin beds, **ask for a** *cama de casal* ("couple's bed"; no wedding ring seems to be required).

The lodgings (all indicated with a 🏨) that we list are the cream of the crop in each price category. We always list the facilities that are available—but we don't specify whether they cost extra: when pricing accommodations, always ask what's included. All hotels listed have private bath unless otherwise noted. Properties indicated by are lodging establishments whose restaurant warrants a special trip.

Assume that hotels operate on the European Plan (**EP**, with no meals) unless we specify that they're all-inclusive (including all meals and most activities) or use the Breakfast Plan (**BP**, with a full breakfast daily), Continental Plan (**CP**, with a Continental breakfast daily), Full American Plan (**FAP**, with all meals), or Modified American Plan (**MAP**, with breakfast and dinner daily).

HOTELS
Hotels listed with EMBRATUR, Brazil's national tourist board, are rated using stars. Note, however, that the number of stars awarded appears to be based strictly on the number of amenities, without taking into account intangibles such as service and atmosphere.

Hotels accept credit cards for payment, but first ask if there's a discount for cash. Try to bargain hard for a cash-on-the barrel discount, then pay in local currency.

Mail & Shipping

Post offices are called *correios*, and branches are marked by the name and a logo that looks something like two interlocked fingers; most are open weekdays 8–5 and Saturday until noon.

Mailboxes are small yellow boxes marked CORREIOS that sit atop metal pedestals on street corners. Airmail from Brazil takes at least 10 or more days to reach the United States, possibly longer to Canada and the United Kingdom, definitely longer to Australia and New Zealand.

➤ **POST OFFICE: Correio** (Praça do Correio, tel. 011/3831–5522).

OVERNIGHT SERVICES

Brazil has both national and international express mail service, the price of which varies according to the weight of the package and the destination. International express mail companies operating out of Brazil include Federal Express and DHL.

➤ **OVERNIGHT SERVICES: DHL** (Rua da Consolação 2721, Jardins, tel. 0800/10–6023). **FedEx** (Av. São Luís 187, Loja 43, Centro, tel. 011/5641–7788).

POSTAL RATES

An airmail letter from Brazil to the United States and most parts of Europe, including the United Kingdom, costs about R$2.16 ($1). Aerograms and postcards cost the same.

RECEIVING MAIL

Mail can be addressed to "poste restante" and sent to any major post office. The address must include the code for that particular branch. American Express will hold mail for its cardholders.

Metrô Travel

The metrô is safe, quick, comfortable, and clean, but unfortunately it doesn't serve many of the city's southern districts. The blue line runs north–south, the orange line runs east–west, and the green line runs under Avenida Paulista from Vila Mariana to the new stations at Sumaré and Vila Madalena, near Avenida Pompéia. The metrô operates daily 5 AM–midnight. Tickets are sold in stations and cost R$1.40 one-way. (You can get discounts on round-trip fares and when you buy 10 tickets at once; note that ticket sellers aren't required to change large bills.) You insert the ticket into the turnstile at the platform entrance, and it's returned to you only if there's unused fare on it still. Transfers within the metrô system are free, and for bus–metrô trips (one bus only), you can buy a *bilhete integração* on buses or at metrô stations for R$2.30. Maps of the metrô system are available from the Departamento de Marketing Institucional, or you can pick up the *Guia São Paulo* at newsstands and bookstores.

➤ **METRÔ INFORMATION: Departamento de Marketing Institucional** (Av. Paulista 1842, 19th floor, tel. 011/283–4933). **Metrô** (tel. 011/286–0111 for general information).

Money Matters

Prices throughout this guide are given for adults. Substantially reduced fees are almost always available for children, students, and senior citizens. For information on taxes, *see* Taxes.

Top hotels in São Paulo go for more than R$430 ($200) a night, and meals can—but do not have to—cost as much. Outside Brazil's two largest cities and Brasília, prices for food and lodging tend to drop considerably. Self-service salad bars where you pay by weight (per kilo, about 2.2 pounds) are inexpensive alternatives everywhere, though be sure to choose carefully among them. Taxis can be pricey. City buses, subways, and long-distance buses are all inexpensive; plane fares aren't.

ATMS

Nearly all the nation's major banks have automated teller machines. MasterCard and Cirrus are rarely accepted (some airport Banco Itau ATMs are linked to Cirrus); Visa and Plus cards are. American Express card holders can make withdrawals at most Bradesco ATMs marked 24 HORAS. To be on the safe side, carry a variety of cards. Note also that if your PIN is more than four digits long and/or uses letters instead of numbers, it might not work; talk to your bank. Finally, for your card to function on some ATMs, you may need to hit a screen command (perhaps, *estrangeiro*) if you are a foreign client.

➤ **ATM LOCATIONS: MasterCard Cirrus** (tel. 800/424–7787). **Visa Plus** (tel. 800/843–7587).

CREDIT CARDS

In Brazil's largest cities and leading tourist centers, restaurants, hotels, and shops accept major international credit cards. Off the beaten track, you may have more difficulty using them. Many gas stations in rural Brazil don't take credit cards.

For costly items use your credit card whenever possible—you'll come out ahead, whether the exchange rate at which your purchase is calculated is the one in effect the day the vendor's bank abroad processes the charge or the one prevailing on the day the charge company's service center processes it at home.

Throughout this guide, the following abbreviations are used: **AE,** American Express; **DC,** Diners Club; **MC,** MasterCard; and **V,** Visa.

CURRENCY

Brazil's unit of currency is the real (R$; plural: *reais*, though it's sometimes seen as *reals*). One real has 100 centavos (cents). There are notes worth 1, 5, 10, 50, and 100 reais, together with coins worth 1, 5, 10, 25, and 50 centavos, and 1 real, all of which feel and look similar.

CURRENCY EXCHANGE

At press time, the real was at 3.56 to the pound sterling, 2.51 to the U.S. dollar, 1.59 to the Canadian dollar, 1.34 to the Australia dollar, and 1.09 to the New Zealand dollar.

For the most favorable rates, **change money through banks.** Although ATM transaction fees may be higher abroad than at home, ATM rates are excellent because they are based on wholesale rates offered only by major banks. You won't do as well at *casas de câmbio* (exchange houses) in airports or rail and bus stations, in hotels, in restaurants, or in stores.

Avenida Paulista is the home of many banks (generally open 10–4), including Citibank. For currency exchange services without any extra fees, try Action. In Centro, you can exchange money at Banco do Brasil and at Banespa. Several banks have automatic-teller machines (ATMs) that accept international bank cards and dispense reais.

To avoid lines at airport exchange booths, **get local currency before you leave home.** (Don't wait until the last minute to do this as many banks—even the international ones—don't have reais on hand and must order them for you. This can take a couple days.) Outside larger cities, changing money in Brazil becomes more of a challenge. It's best when leaving a large city for a smaller town to travel with enough cash. For an average week in a Brazilian city, a good strategy is to convert $500 into reais. This provides sufficient cash for most expenses, such as taxis and small purchases and snacks.

➤ **BANKS: Banco do Brasil** (Av. São João 32, Centro, tel. 011/234–1646). **Banespa** (Rua Duque de Caxias 200, República, tel. 011/222–7722). **Citibank** (Av. Paulista 1111, Jardins, tel. 011/5576–1190).

➤ **EXCHANGE SERVICE: Action** (Guarulhos Airport, TPS2 arrival floor, tel. 011/6445–4458; Rua Melo Alves 357, Jardins, tel. 011/3064–2910; Shopping Paulista, Rua 13 de Maio 1947, Paraíso, tel. 011/288–4222).

Packing

If you're doing business in Brazil, you'll need the same attire you would wear in U.S. and European cities: for men, suits and ties; for women, suits for day wear and cocktail dresses or the like for an evening out. For sightseeing, casual clothing and good walking shoes are appropriate; most restaurants don't require very formal attire. For beach vacations, you'll need lightweight sportswear, a bathing suit, a beach cover-up, a sun hat, and really good sunscreen.

Passports & Visas

When traveling internationally, **carry your passport** even if you don't need one (it's always the best form of I.D.) and **make two photocopies of the data page** (one for someone at home and another for you, carried separately from your passport). If you lose your passport, promptly call the nearest embassy or consulate and the local police.

ENTERING BRAZIL

To enter Brazil, all U.S. citizens, even infants, must have both a passport and a tourist visa (valid for five years). To obtain one, you must submit the following to the Brazilian embassy or to the nearest consulate: a passport that will be valid for six months past the date of first entry to Brazil; a passport-type photo; a photocopy of your round-trip ticket or a signed letter from a travel agency with confirmed round-trip bookings or proof of your ability to pay for your stay in Brazil; and cash, a money order, or a certified check for $45 (there's also a $10 handling fee if anyone other than the applicant submits the visa).

If you're a business traveler, you may need a business visa (valid for 90 days). It has all the same requirements as a tourist visa, but you'll also need a letter on company letterhead—addressed to the embassy or consulate and signed by an authorized representative (other than you)—stating the nature of your business in Brazil, itinerary, business contacts, dates of arrival and departure, and that the company assumes all financial and moral responsibility while you're in Brazil. The fee is $105 (plus the $10 fee if someone other than you submits the visa). In addition to the forms of payment detailed above, a company check is also acceptable.

Canadian nationals, Australians, and New Zealanders also need visas to enter the country. For Canadians, the fee is US$40; for New Zealanders, US$20; and for Australians, there's no charge. Citizens of the United Kingdom don't need a visa.

In the United States there are consulates in Atlanta, Boston, Chicago, Houston, Los Angeles, Miami, New York, San Francisco, and San Juan. To get the location of the Brazilian consulate to which you must apply, contact the Brazilian embassy. Note that some consulates don't allow you to apply for a visa by mail. If you don't live near a city with a consulate, consider hiring a concierge-type service to do your legwork. Many cities have these companies, which not only help with the paperwork for such things as visas and passports but also send someone to wait in line for you.

Rest Rooms

The word for "bathroom" is *banheiro*, though the term *sanitários* (toilets) is also used. *Homens* means "men" and *mulheres* means "women." Around major tourist attractions and along the main beaches in big cities, you'll find public rest rooms. In other areas you may have to rely on the kindness of local restaurant and shop owners. If a smile and polite request ("*Por favor, posso usar o banheiro?*") don't work, become a customer—the purchase of a drink or a knickknack might just buy you a trip to the bathroom. Rest areas with relatively clean, well-equipped bathrooms are plentiful along major highways. Still, carry a pocket-size package of tissues in case there's no toilet paper. Bathroom attendants will truly appreciate a tip of a few spare centavos.

Safety

Stay alert and guard your belongings at all times, especially at major sights. Avoid wearing shorts, expensive running shoes, or flashy jewelry—all of which attract attention. Also beware of the local scam in which one person throws a dark liquid on you and another offers to help you clean up while the first really cleans up!

Avoid flashing money around. To safeguard your funds, **lock traveler's checks and cash in a hotel safe**, except for what you need to carry each day. Money (and important documents) that you do carry are best tucked into a money belt or carried in the inside pockets of your clothing. Wear the simplest of timepieces and **do not wear any jewelry you aren't willing to lose**—stories of thieves yanking chains or earrings off travelers aren't uncommon. **Keep cameras in a secure camera bag,** preferably one with a chain or wire embedded in the strap. Always **remain alert for pickpockets,** particularly in market areas, and **follow local advice about where it's safe to walk.**

Note that Brazilian law requires everyone to have official identification with them at all times. Carry a copy of your passport's data page and of the Brazilian visa stamp (leave the actual passport in the hotel safe).

LOCAL SCAMS

Most tourist-related crimes occur in busy public areas: beaches, sidewalks or plazas, bus stations (and on buses, too). In these settings, pickpockets, usually young children, work in groups. One or more will try to distract you while another grabs a wallet, bag, or camera. **Beware of children who suddenly thrust themselves in front of you** to ask for money or who offer to shine your shoes. Another member of the gang may strike from behind, grab whatever valuable is available, and disappear in the crowd. It's best not to protest if you're mugged. Those on the take are sometimes armed or will tell you that their backup is, and although they're often quite young, they can be dangerous.

WOMEN IN BRAZIL

Although women are gradually assuming a more important role in the nation's job force, machismo is still a strong part of Brazilian culture. Stares and catcalls aren't uncommon. Although you should have no fear of traveling unaccompanied, you should still take a few precautions.

Ask your hotel staff to recommend a reliable cab company, and **call for a taxi instead of hailing one on the street,** especially at night. **Dress to avoid unwanted attention.** For example, always wear a cover-up when heading to or from the beach. **Avoid eye** contact with unsavory individuals. If such a person approaches you, discourage him by politely but firmly by saying, "*Por favor, me dê licença*" ("Excuse me, please") and then walk away with resolve.

Senior-Citizen Travel

There's no reason why active, well-traveled senior citizens shouldn't visit Brazil, whether on an independent (but prebooked) vacation, an escorted tour, or an adventure vacation. The country is full of good hotels and competent ground operators who will meet your flights and organize your sightseeing. Before you leave home, however, determine what medical services your health insurance will cover outside the United States; note that Medicare doesn't provide for payment of hospital and medical services outside the United States. If you need additional travel insurance, buy it.

To qualify for age-related discounts, **mention your senior-citizen status up front** when booking hotel reservations (not when checking out) and before you're seated in restaurants (not when paying the bill). When renting a car, ask about promotional car-rental discounts, which can be cheaper than senior-citizen rates.

Sightseeing Tours

You can hire a bilingual guide through a travel agency or hotel concierge (about R$15 an hour with a four-hour minimum), or you can design your own walking tour with the aid of information provided at Anhembi booths around the city. Anhembi also offers Sunday tours of museums, parks, and Centro that are less expensive than those offered in hotels. The tourist board offers three different half-day Sunday bus tours: of the parks, of the museums, and of historic downtown. Officially, none of their guides speaks English; however, they may be able to arrange something on request.

Gol Tour Viagens e Turismo and Opcional Tour and Guide Viagens e Turismo offer custom tours as well as car tours for small groups. A half-day city tour costs about R$40 a person (group rate); a night tour—including a samba show, dinner, and drinks—costs around R$100; and day trips to the beach or the colonial city of Embu cost R$80–R$90. The English-speaking staff at Savoy specializes in personalized tours.

Canoar is one of the best rafting tour operators in São Paulo State. Trilha Brazil arranges treks in forests around São Paulo. Reputable operators that offer rain-forest, beach, and island excursions include Biotrip, Pisa Trekking, and Venturas e Aventuras.

►TOUR-OPERATOR RECOMMENDATIONS: Biotrip (Rua Gama Cerqueira 187, Cambuci, tel. 011/278–1122). Canoar (Rua Caetés 410, Sumaré, tel. 011/3871–2282). Gol Tour Viagens e Turismo (Av. São Luís 187, Basement, Loja 12, Centro, tel. 011/256–2388). Opcional Tour and Guide Viagens e Turismo (Av. Ipiranga 345, 14th floor, Suite 1401, Centro, tel. 011/259–1007). Pisa Trekking (Alameda dos Tupiniquins 202, Moema, tel. 011/5571–2525). Savoy (Rua James Watt 142, Suite 92, Itaim Bibi, tel. 011/5507–2064 or 011/5507–2065). Tourist board (tel. 011/6971–5000). Trilha Brazil (Rua Professor Rubião Meira 86, Jardim América, tel. 011/3082–7089). Venturas e Aventuras (Rua Minerva 268, Perdizes, tel. 011/3872–0362).

Taxes

Sales tax is included in the prices shown on goods in stores. Hotel, meal, and car rental taxes are usually tacked on in addition to the costs shown on menus and brochures. At press time, hotel taxes were roughly 5%; meal taxes, 10%; car rental taxes, 12%.

Departure taxes on international flights from Brazil aren't always included in your ticket and can run as high as R$86 ($34); domestic flights may incur a R$22 ($9) tax. Although U.S. dollars are accepted in some airports, be prepared to **pay departure taxes in reais.**

Taxis

Taxis in São Paulo are white. Owner-driven taxis are generally well maintained and reliable as are radio taxis. Fares start at R\$3.40 and run R\$.75 for each kilometer (½ mi) or R\$.40 for every minute sitting in traffic. After 8 PM and on weekends fares rise by 20%. You'll also pay a tax if the taxi leaves the city, as is the case with trips to Cumbica Airport. Good radio-taxi companies include Chame Taxi, Ligue-Taxi, and Paulista.

➤ **TAXI COMPANIES: Chame Taxi** (tel. 011/3865–3033). **Ligue-Taxi** (tel. 011/3672–2633). **Paulista** (tel. 011/3746–6555).

Telephones

Phone booths are bright green and yellow. Most operate using prepaid cards, but some still use tokens. Both cards and tokens are sold at newsstands. Cards with 30 credits are sold for R\$3. Each credit allows you to talk for 3 minutes on local calls and 17 seconds on long-distance calls.

International calls can be made at special phone booths found in Telesp offices around the city. You can choose your own long-distance company. After dialing 0, dial a two-digit company code, followed by the country code and/or area code and number. To call Rio, for example, dial 0, then 21 (for Embratel, a major long-distance and international provider), then 21 (Rio's area code), and then the number. To call the United States, dial 00 (for international calls), 23 (for Intelig, another long-distance company), 1 (country code), and the area code and phone number. For operator-assisted (in English) international calls, dial 000111. To make a collect long-distance call (which will cost 40% more than normal calls), dial 9 + the area code and the number. São Paulo's area code is 11; phone numbers in the city and state have six, seven, or eight digits. Most cellular phone numbers have eight digits (a few have seven) and start with the number 9.

COUNTRY & AREA CODES

To call Brazil from overseas, dial the country code, 55, and then the area code, omitting the first 0. The area code for Rio is 021, for São Paulo, 011. Other area codes are listed in the front of local phone directories and in chapter A to Z sections throughout this guide.

DIRECTORY & OPERATOR INFORMATION

For local directory assistance, dial 102. For directory assistance in another Brazilian city, dial the area code of that city plus 121.

LONG-DISTANCE SERVICES

AT&T, MCI, and Sprint access codes make calling long distance relatively convenient, but you may find the local access number blocked in many hotel rooms. First ask the hotel operator to connect you. If the hotel operator balks, ask for an international operator, or dial the international operator yourself. One way to improve your odds of getting connected to your long-distance carrier is to travel with more than one company's calling card (a hotel may block Sprint, for example, but not MCI). If all else fails, call from a pay phone.

Time

Although Brazil technically covers several time zones, most Brazilian cities are three hours behind GMT (Greenwich mean time), which means that if it's 5 PM in London, it's 2 PM in Rio and noon in New York.

Tipping

Note that wages can be paltry, so a little generosity can go a long way. At hotels, it can go even farther if you tip in U.S. dollars or pounds sterling (bills, not coins). At restaurants that add a 10% service charge onto the check, it's customary to give the waiter an additional 5% tip. If there's no service charge, leave 15%. In deluxe hotels, tip porters R$2 (75¢) per bag, chambermaids R$2 (75¢) per day, bellhops R$4–R$6 ($1.50–$2.50) for room and valet service. Tips for doormen and concierges vary, depending on the services provided; a good tip would be R$22 ($9) or higher, average R$11 ($4). For moderate and inexpensive hotels, tips tend to be minimal (salaries are so low that virtually anything is well received). If a taxi driver helps you with your luggage, a per-bag charge of about 75 centavos (30¢) is levied in addition to the fare. In general, tip taxi drivers 10% of the fare.

At the barber shop or beauty salon, a 10%–20% tip is expected. If a service station attendant does anything beyond filling up the gas tank, leave him a small tip of some spare change. Tipping in bars and cafés follows the rules of restaurants, although at outdoor bars Brazilians rarely leave a gratuity if they had only a soft drink or a beer. At airports and at train and bus stations, tip the last porter who puts your bags into the cab (R$1/50¢ a bag at airports, 50 centavos (20¢) a bag at bus and train stations). In large cities, you'll often be accosted on the street by children looking for handouts; 50 centavos (20¢) is an average "tip."

Tours & Packages

Because everything is prearranged on a prepackaged tour or independent vacation, you spend less time planning—and often get it all at a good price.

BOOKING WITH AN AGENT

Travel agents are excellent resources. But it's a good idea to collect brochures from several agencies as some agents' suggestions may be influenced by relationships with tour and package firms that reward them for volume sales. If you have a special interest, **find an agent with expertise in that area** the American Society of Travel Agents (ASTA; ☞ Travel Agencies) has a database of specialists worldwide.

Make sure your travel agent knows the accommodations and other services of the place they're recommending. Ask about the hotel's location, room size, beds, and whether it has a pool, room service, or programs for children, if you care about these. Has your agent been there in person or sent others whom you can contact?

Do some homework on your own, too: local tourism boards can provide information about lesser-known and small-niche operators, some of which may sell only direct.

BUYER BEWARE

Each year consumers are stranded or lose their money when tour operators—even large ones with excellent reputations—go out of business. So check out the operator. Ask several travel agents about its reputation, and try to book with a company that has a consumer-protection program. (Look for information in the company's brochure.) In the United States, members of the National Tour Association and the United States Tour Operators Association are required to set aside funds to cover your payments and travel arrangements in the event that the company defaults. It's also a good idea to choose a company that participates in the American Society of Travel Agents' Tour Operator Program (TOP); ASTA will act as mediator in any disputes between you and your tour operator.

Remember that the more your package or tour includes the better you can predict the ultimate cost of your vacation. Make sure you know exactly what is covered, and beware of hidden costs. Are taxes, tips, and transfers included? Entertainment and excursions? These can add up.

➤ **TOUR-OPERATOR RECOMMENDATIONS: American Society of Travel Agents** (☞ Travel Agencies). **National Tour Association** (NTA; 546 E. Main St., Lexington, KY 40508, tel. 859/226–4444 or 800/682–8886, www.ntaonline.com). **United States Tour Operators Association** (USTOA; 342 Madison Ave., Suite 1522, New York, NY 10173, tel. 212/599–6599 or 800/468–7862, fax 212/599–6744, www.ustoa.com).

Train Travel

Most travel to the interior of the state is done by bus or automobile. Still, a few places are served by trains. Trains from Estação da Luz, near 25 de Março, run to some metropolitan suburbs and small interior towns. Trains from Estação Barra Funda serve towns in the west of the state. Estação Júlio Prestes, in Campos Eliseos, has trains to the southeast and some suburbs. Estação Roosevelt serves the suburbs only.

➤ **TRAIN INFORMATION: Estação Barra Funda** (Rua Mário de Andrade 664, Barra Funda, tel. 011/3612–1527). **Estação Júlio Prestes** (Praça Júlio Prestes 148, Campos Elíseos, tel. 011/220–8862). **Estação da Luz** (Praça da Luz 1, Luz, tel. 011/227–7605). **Estação Roosevelt** (Praça Agente Cícero, Brás, tel. 011/266–4455).

Travel Agencies

A good travel agent puts your needs first. Look for an agency that has been in business at least five years, emphasizes customer service, and has someone on staff who specializes in your destination. In addition, **make sure the agency belongs to a professional trade organization.** The American Society of Travel Agents (ASTA)—the largest and most influential in the field with more than 26,000 members in some 170 countries—maintains and enforces a strict code of ethics and will step in to help mediate any agent-client disputes if necessary. ASTA (whose motto is "Without a travel agent, you're on your own") also maintains a Web site that includes a directory of agents. (If a travel agency is also acting as your tour operator, *see* Buyer Beware in Tours & Packages.)

➤ **LOCAL AGENT REFERRALS: American Society of Travel Agents** (ASTA; tel. 800/965–2782 24-hr hot line, fax 703/739–7642, www.astanet.com). **Association of British Travel Agents** (68–71 Newman St., London W1T 3AH, U.K., tel. 020/7637–2444, fax 020/7637–0713, www.abtanet.com). **Association of Canadian Travel Agents** (130 Albert St., Ste. 1705, Ottawa, Ontario K1P

5G4, Canada, tel. 613/237–3657, fax 613/237–7502, www.acta.net).
Australian Federation of Travel Agents (Level 3, 309 Pitt St.,
Sydney NSW 2000, Australia, tel. 02/9264–3299, fax 02/9264–1085,
www.afta.com.au). **Travel Agents' Association of New Zealand**
(Box 1888, Wellington 10033, New Zealand, tel. 04/499–0104,
fax 04/499–0827, www.taanz.org.nz).

Visitor Information

The most helpful contact is the São Paulo Convention and
Visitors Bureau, open 9–6. The sharp, business-minded director,
Roberto Gheler, speaks English flawlessly and is extremely
knowledgeable. Branches of the city-operated Anhembi Turismo
e Eventos da Cidade de São Paulo are open daily 9–6.

The bureaucracy-laden Secretaria de Esportes e Turismo do
Estado de São Paulo, open weekdays 9–6, has maps and
information about the city and state of São Paulo. SEST also has
a booth at the arrivals terminal in Cumbica airport; it's open
daily 9 AM–10 PM.

➤ **TOURIST INFORMATION: Anhembi Turismo e Eventos da
Cidade de São Paulo** (Anhembi Convention Center, Av. Olavo
Fontoura 1209, Santana, tel. 011/6971–5000; Praça da República
at Rua 7 de Abril, Centro, tel. 011/231–2922; Av. São Luís at Praça
Dom José Gaspar, Centro, tel. 011/257–3422); Av. Paulista, across
from MASP, Cerqueira César, tel. 011/251–0970; Av. Brigadeiro Faria
Lima, in front of Shopping Center Iguatemi, Jardim Paulista, tel.
011/3031–1277). **São Paulo Convention and Visitors Bureau** (Rua
Dom José de Barros 17, Centro, tel. 011/289–7588). **Secretaria de
Esportes e Turismo do Estado de São Paulo** (SEST; Praça Antônio
Prado 9, Centro, tel. 011/239–5822).

When to Go

CLIMATE
Seasons below the equator are the reverse of the north—
summer in Brazil runs from December to March and winter from

June to September. The rainy season in Brazil occurs during the summer months, but this is rarely a nuisance. Showers can be torrential but usually last no more than an hour or two. The areas of the country with pronounced rainy seasons are the Amazon and the Pantanal. In these regions, the rainy season runs roughly from November to May and is marked by heavy, twice-daily downpours.

In the south, São Paulo, and parts of Minas Gerais, winter temperatures can fall to the low 40s (5°C–8°C). In the southern states of Santa Catarina and Rio Grande do Sul, snowfalls occur in winter, although they're seldom more than dustings.

► **FORECASTS: Weather Channel Connection** (tel. 900/932–8437), 95¢ per minute from a Touch-Tone phone.

The following are the average daily maximum and minimum temperatures for São Paolo.

Jan.	84F	29C	May	77F	25C	Sept.	75F	24C
	69	21		66	19		66	19
Feb.	85F	29C	June	76F	24C	Oct.	77F	25C
	73	23		64	18		63	17
Mar.	83F	28C	July	75F	24C	Nov.	79F	26C
	72	22		64	18		68	20
Apr.	80F	27C	Aug.	76F	24C	Dec.	82F	28C
	69	21		64	18		71	22

FESTIVALS AND SEASONAL EVENTS
Note that country-wide events and celebrations related to Brazil's biggest festival, Carnaval, start in January and peak in the days preceding Lent, sometime in February or March. Remember: the country's seasons are the reverse of those in the northern hemisphere.

► **MAY:** Many communities throughout Brazil celebrate the **Festa do Divino Espírito Santo**, with food donations for the poor, processionals, and folklore festivals.

➤ **JUNE:** In São Paulo, the annual **Carlton Dance Festival** starts in June and continues through July.

➤ **JULY:** The **Festival de Inverno,** in Campos do Jordão, São Paulo, is one of Brazil's most important classical musical events. Young musicians can learn from more experienced ones, and everyone can watch performances at the Auditório Cláudio Santoro.

➤ **AUG.:** São Paulo's Museu da Imagem e do Som sponsors the **International Short Film Festival** in August. The month also sees the city's annual, three-day **Free Jazz Festival.**

➤ **OCT.:** Not only is October 12 the official day (celebrated all over the country and particularly in Aparecida in São Paulo State) of Brazil's patron saint, **Nossa Senhora da Aparecida,** but it's also **Children's Day.** São Paulo's international film festival, **Mostra Internacional de Cinema,** is held in October. The world-renowned biennial art exhibition (South America's largest), the **São Paulo Biennial,** is held from mid-October to mid-December in each even-numbered year in Ibirapuera Park.

➤ **MARCH: The Formula I Grand Prix** is held during March in São Paulo.

➤ **APRIL:** April 21 is **Tiradentes Day,** a national holiday honoring the father of Brazil's 18th-century independence movement, the Inconfidência. On this date, Joaquim José da Silva Xavier, known as Tiradentes (Tooth Puller) because he was a dentist, was executed for treason by the Portuguese crown in Ouro Preto. The city celebrates over a four-day period (April 18–21) with many ceremonies.

Your checklist for a perfect journey

WAY AHEAD

- Devise a trip budget.

- Write down the five things you want most from this trip. Keep this list handy before and during your trip.

- Make plane or train reservations. Book lodging and rental cars.

- Arrange for pet care.

- Check your passport. Apply for a new one if necessary.

- Photocopy important documents and store in a safe place.

A MONTH BEFORE

- Make restaurant reservations and buy theater and concert tickets. Visit fodors.com for links to local events.

- Familiarize yourself with the local language or lingo.

TWO WEEKS BEFORE

- Replenish your supply of medications.

- Create your itinerary.

- Enjoy a book or movie set in your destination to get you in the mood.

- Develop a packing list. Shop for missing essentials. Repair and launder or dry-clean your clothes.

A WEEK BEFORE

- Stop newspaper deliveries. Pay bills.

- Acquire traveler's checks.

- Stock up on film.

- Label your luggage.

- Finalize your packing list— take less than you think you need.

- Create a toiletries kit filled with travel-size essentials.

- Get lots of sleep. Don't get sick before your trip.

A DAY BEFORE

- Drink plenty of water.

- Check your travel documents.

- Get packing!

DURING YOUR TRIP

- Keep a journal/scrapbook.

- Spend time with locals.

- Take time to explore. Don't plan too much.

WORDS AND PHRASES

English	Portuguese	Pronunciation

Basics

English	Portuguese	Pronunciation
Yes/no	Sim/Não	**see**ing/nown
Please	Por favor	pohr fah-**vohr**
May I?	Posso?	**poh**-sso
Thank you (very much)	(Muito) obrigado	(**mooyn**-too) o-bree **gah**-doh
You're welcome	De nada	day **nah**-dah
Excuse me	Com licença	con lee-**ssehn**-ssah
Pardon me/what did you say?	Desculpe/O que disse?	des-**kool**-peh/o.k. dih-say?
Could you tell me?	Poderia me dizer?	po-day-**ree**-ah mee dee-**zehr**?
I'm sorry	Sinto muito	**seen**-too **mooyn**-too
Good morning!	Bom dia!	bohn **dee**-ah
Good afternoon!	Boa tarde!	**boh**-ah **tahr**-dee
Good evening!	Boa noite!	**boh**-äh **nohee**-tee
Goodbye!	Adeus!/Até logo!	ah-**dehoos**/ah-**teh loh**-go
Mr./Mrs.	Senhor/Senhora	sen-**yor**/sen-**yohr**-ah
Miss	Senhorita	sen-yo-**ri**-tah
Pleased to meet you	Muito prazer	**mooyn**-too prah-**zehr**
How are you?	Como vai?	**koh**-mo **vah**-ee
Very well, thank you	Muito bem, obri-gado	**mooyn**-too **beh**-in o-bree-**gah**-doh
And you?	E o(a) Senhor(a)?	eh oh sen-**yor** (**yohr**-ah)
Hello (on the telephone)	Alô	ah-**low**

Numbers

1	um/uma	oom/oom-ah
2	dois	dohees
3	três	trehys
4	quatro	kwa-troh
5	cinco	seen-koh
6	seis	sehys
7	sete	seh-tee
8	oito	ohee-too
9	nove	noh-vee
10	dez	deh-ees
11	onze	ohn-zee
12	doze	doh-zee
13	treze	treh-zee
14	quatorze	kwa-tohr-zee
15	quinze	keen-zee
16	dezesseis	deh-zeh-sehys
17	dezessete	deh-zeh-seh-tee
18	dezoito	deh-zohee-toh
19	dezenove	deh-zeh-noh-vee
20	vinte	veen-tee
21	vinte e um	veen-tee eh oom
30	trinta	treen-tah
32	trinta e dois	treen-ta eh dohees
40	quarenta	kwa-rehn-ta
43	quarenta e três	kwa-rehn-ta e trehys
50	cinquenta	seen-kwehn-tah
54	cinquenta e quatro	seen-kwehn-tah e kwa-troh
60	sessenta	seh-sehn-tah
65	sessenta e cinco	seh-sehn-tah e seen-ko
70	setenta	seh-tehn-tah
76	setenta e seis	seh-tehn-ta e sehys
80	oitenta	ohee-tehn-ta
87	oitenta e sete	ohee-tehn-ta e seh-tee
90	noventa	noh-vehn-ta

98	noventa e oito	noh-**vehn**-ta e **ohee**-too
100	cem	**seh**-ing
101	cento e um	**sehn**-too e **oom**
200	duzentos	doo-**zehn**-tohss
500	quinhentos	key-**nyehn**-tohss
700	setecentos	seh-teh-**sehn**-tohss
900	novecentos	noh-veh-**sehn**-tohss
1,000	mil	meel
2,000	dois mil	**dohees** meel
1,000,000	um milhão	oom mee-lee-**ahon**

Colors

black	preto	**preh**-toh
blue	azul	a-**zool**
brown	marrom	mah-**hohm**
green	verde	**vehr**-deh
pink	rosa	**roh**-zah
purple	roxo	**roh**-choh
orange	laranja	lah-**rahn**-jah
red	vermelho	vehr-**meh**-lyoh
white	branco	**brahn**-coh
yellow	amarelo	ah-mah-**reh**-loh

Days of the Week

Sunday	Domingo	doh-**meehn**-goh
Monday	Segunda-feira	seh-**goon**-dah **fey**-rah
Tuesday	Terça-feira	**tehr**-sah **fey**-rah
Wednesday	Quarta-feira	**kwahr**-tah **fey**-rah
Thursday	Quinta-feira	**keen**-tah **fey**-rah
Friday	Sexta-feira	**sehss**-tah **fey**-rah
Saturday	Sábado	**sah**-bah-doh

Months

January	Janeiro	jah-**ney**-roh
February	Fevereiro	feh-veh-**rey**-roh
March	Março	**mahr**-soh

April	Abril	ah-**breel**
May	Maio	**my**-oh
June	Junho	gyoo-**nyoh**
July	Julho	gyoo-**lyoh**
August	Agosto	ah-**ghost**-toh
September	Setembro	seh-**tehm**-broh
October	Outubro	owe-**too**-broh
November	Novembro	noh-**vehm**-broh
December	Dezembro	deh-**zehm**-broh

Useful Phrases

Do you speak English?	O Senhor fala inglês?	oh sen-**yor fah**-lah een-**glehs**?
I don't speak Portuguese.	Não falo português.	nown **fah**-loh pohr-too-**ghehs**
I don't understand (you)	Não lhe entendo	nown lyeh ehn-**tehn**-doh
I understand	Eu entendo	**eh**-oo ehn-**tehn**-doh
I don't know	Não sei	nown say
I am American/ British	Sou americano (americana)/ inglês/inglêsa	sow a-meh-ree-**cah**-noh (a-meh-ree-**cah**-nah/ een-**glehs**(een-**glah**-sa)
What's your name?	Como se chama?	**koh**-moh seh **shah**-mah
My name is . . .	Meu nome é . . .	mehw **noh**-meh eh
What time is it?	Que horas são?	keh **oh**-rahss **sa**-ohn
It is one, two, three . . . o'clock	É uma/São duas, três . . . hora/horas	eh **oom**-ah/**sa**-ohn **oo**mah, **doo**-ahss, **treh**ys oh-rah/oh-rahs
Yes, please/No, thank you	Sim por favor/ Não obrigado	seing pohr fah-**vohr**/ nown o-bree-**gah**-doh
How?	Como?	**koh**-moh
When?	Quando?	**kwahn**-doh
This/Next week	Esta/Próxima semana	**ehss**-tah/**proh**-see-mah seh-**mah**-nah
This/Next month	Este/Próximo mêz	**ehss**-teh/**proh**-see-moh mehz

This/Next year	Este/Próximo ano	ehss-teh/proh-see-moh ah-noh
Yesterday/today tomorrow	Ontem/hoje amanhã	ohn-tehn/oh-jeh/ ah-mah-nyan
This morning/ afternoon	Esta manhã/ tarde	ehss-tah mah-nyan / tahr-deh
Tonight	Hoje a noite	oh-jeh ah nohee-tee
What?	O que?	oh keh
What is it?	O que é isso?	oh keh eh ee-soh
Why?	Por quê?	pohr-keh
Who?	Quem?	keh-in
Where is . . . ?	Onde é . . . ?	ohn-deh eh
the train station?	a estação de trem?	ah es-tah-sah-on deh train
the subway station?	a estação de metrô?	ah es-tah-sah-on deh meh-tro
the bus stop?	a parada do ônibus?	ah pah-rah-dah doh oh-nee-boos
the post office?	o correio?	oh coh-hay-yoh
the bank?	o banco?	oh bahn-koh
the hotel?	o hotel . . . ?	oh oh-tell
the cashier?	o caixa?	oh kahy-shah
the museum?	o museo . . . ?	oh moo-zeh-oh
the hospital?	o hospital?	oh ohss-pee-tal
the elevator?	o elevador?	oh eh-leh-vah-dohr
the bathroom?	o banheiro?	oh bahn-yey-roh
the beach?	a praia de . . . ?	ah prahy-yah deh
Here/there	Aqui/ali	ah-kee/ah-lee
Open/closed	Aberto/fechado	ah-behr-toh/feh-shah-doh
Left/right	Esquerda/ direita	ehs-kehr-dah/ dee-ray-tah
Straight ahead	Em frente	ehyn frehn-teh
Is it near/far?	É perto/longe?	eh pehr-toh/lohn-jeh
I'd like to buy . . .	Gostaria de comprar . . .	gohs-tah-ree-ah deh cohm-prahr . . .
a bathing suit	um maiô	oom mahy-owe

a dictionary	um dicionário	oom dee-seeoh-**nah**-reeoh
a hat	um chapéu	oom shah-**pehoo**
a magazine	uma revista	**oo**mah heh-**vees**-tah
a map	um mapa	oom **mah**-pah
a postcard	cartão postal	kahr-**town** pohs-**tahl**
sunglasses	óculos escuros	ah-koo-loss ehs-**koo**-rohs
suntan lotion bronzear	um óleo de brohn-zeh-**ahr**	oom **oh**-lyoh deh
a ticket	um bilhete	oom bee-**lyeh**-teh
cigarettes	cigarros	see-**gah**-hose
envelopes	envelopes	eyn-veh-**loh**-pehs
matches	fósforos	**fohs**-foh-rohss
paper	papel	pah-**pehl**
sandals	sandália	sahn-**dah**-leeah
soap	sabonete	sah-bow-**neh**-teh
How much is it?	Quanto custa?	**kwahn**-too **koos**-tah
It's expensive/ cheap	Está caro/ barato	ehss-**tah kah**-roh / bah-**rah**-toh
A little/a lot	Um pouco/muito	oom **pohw**-koh/ **mooyn**-too
More/less	Mais/menos	**mah**-ees /**meh**-nohss
Enough/too much/too little	Suficiente/ demais/ muito pouco	soo-fee-see-**ehn**-teh/ deh-**mah**-ees/ **mooyn**-toh **pohw**-koh
Telephone	Telefone	teh-leh-**foh**-neh
Telegram	Telegrama	teh-leh-**grah**-mah
I am ill.	Estou doente.	ehss-**tow** doh-**ehn**-teh
Please call a doctor.	Por favor chame um médico.	pohr fah-**vohr shah**-meh oom **meh**-dee-koh
Help!	Socorro!	soh-**koh**-ho
Help me!	Me ajude!	mee ah-**jyew**-deh
Fire!	Incêndio!	een-**sehn**-deeoh
Caution!/Look out!/ Be careful!	Cuidado!	kooy-**dah**-doh

On the Road

Avenue	Avenida	ah-veh-**nee**-dah
Highway	Estrada	ehss-**trah**-dah
Port	Porto	**pohr**-toh
Service station	Posto de gasolina	**pohs**-toh deh gah-zoh-**lee**-nah
Street	Rua	**who**-ah
Toll	Pedagio	peh-**dah**-jyoh
Waterfront promenade	Beiramar/ orla	behy-rah-**mahrr**/ **ohr**-lah
Wharf	Cais	**kah**-ees

In Town

Block	Quarteirão	kwahr-tehy-**rah**-on
Cathedral	Catedral	kah-teh-**drahl**
Church/temple	Igreja	ee-**greh**-jyah
City hall	Prefeitura	preh-fehy-**too**-rah
Door/gate	Porta/portão	**pohr**-tah/porh-**tah**-on
Entrance/exit	Entrada/ saída	ehn-**trah**-dah/ sah-ee-dah
Market	Mercado/feira	mehr-**kah**-doh/ **fey**-rah
Neighborhood	Bairro	**buy**-ho
Rustic bar	Lanchonete	lahn-shoh-**neh**-teh
Shop	Loja	**loh**-jyah
Square	Praça	**prah**-ssah

Dining Out

A bottle of . . .	Uma garrafa de . . .	**oo**mah gah-**hah**-fah deh
A cup of . . .	Uma xícara de . . .	**oo**mah **shee**-kah-rah deh
A glass of . . .	Um copo de . . .	oom **koh**-poh deh
Ashtray	Um cinzeiro	oom seen-**zehy**-roh
Bill/check	A conta	ah **kohn**-tah
Bread	Pão	**pah**-on
Breakfast	Café da manhã	kah-**feh** dah mah-**nyan**

Butter	A manteiga	ah mahn-**tehy**-gah
Cheers!	Saúde!	sah-**oo**-deh
Cocktail	Um aperitivo	oom ah-peh-ree-**tee**-voh
Dinner	O jantar	oh **jyahn**-tahr
Dish	Um prato	oom **prah**-toh
Enjoy!	Bom apetite!	bohm ah-peh-**tee**-teh
Fork	Um garfo	**gahr**-foh
Fruit	Fruta	**froo**-tah
Is the tip included?	A gorjeta esta incluída?	ah gohr-**jyeh**-tah ehss-**tah** een-clue-**ee**-dah
Juice	Um suco	oom **soo**-koh
Knife	Uma faca	**oo**mah **fah**-kah
Lunch	O almoço	oh ahl-**moh**-ssoh
Menu	Menu/cardápio	me-**noo** /kahr-**dah**-peeoh
Mineral water	Água mineral	**ah**-gooah mee-neh-**rahl**
Napkin	Guardanapo	gooahr-dah-**nah**-poh
No smoking	Não fumante	nown foo-**mahn**-teh
Pepper	Pimenta	pee-**mehn**-tah
Please give me	Por favor me dê	pohr fah-**vohr** mee **deh**
Salt	Sal	sahl
Smoking	Fumante	foo-**mahn**-teh
Spoon	Uma colher	**oo**mah koh-**lyehr**
Sugar	Açúcar	ah-**soo**-kahr
Waiter!	Garçon!	gahr-**sohn**
Water	Água	**ah**-gooah
Wine	Vinho	**vee**-nyoh

index

FODOR'S POCKET SÃO PAULO

EDITORS: Carissa Bluestone, Lisa Dunford, Laura M. Kidder

Editorial Contributors: Karla Brunet, Joyce Dalton

Editorial Production: Taryn Luciani

Maps: David Lindroth, *cartographer;* Bob Blake and Rebecca Baer, *map editors*

Design: Fabrizio La Rocca, *creative director;* Tigist Getachew, *art director;* Jolie Novak, *senior picture editor;* Melanie Marin, *photo editor*

Production/Manufacturing: Angela L. McLean

Cover Photograph: Yann Arthus-Bertrand/Corbis

COPYRIGHT

First Edition

ISBN 0–676–90212–X

ISSN 1537–7601

IMPORTANT TIP

Although all prices, opening times, and other details in this book are based on information supplied to us at press time, changes occur all the time in the travel world, and Fodor's cannot accept responsibility for facts that become outdated or for inadvertent errors or omissions. So **always confirm information when it matters,** especially if you're making a detour to visit a specific place.

Special Sales

PRINTED IN THE UNITED STATES OF AMERICA

10 9 8 7 6 5 4 3 2 1